Abstracts from the
Land Records of
Dorchester County,
Maryland

Volume A

Liber Old No. 1 to
Liber Old No. 4

1669–1690

James A. McAllister, Jr.

HERITAGE BOOKS
2025

HERITAGE BOOKS

AN IMPRINT OF HERITAGE BOOKS, INC.

Books, CDs, and more—Worldwide

For our listing of thousands of titles see our website
at
www.HeritageBooks.com

A Facsimile Reprint
Published 2021 by
HERITAGE BOOKS, INC.
Publishing Division
5810 Ruatan Street
Berwyn Heights, Md. 20740

Heritage Books by the author:

Abstracts from the Land Records of Dorchester County, Maryland

Volume A: 1669–1690	*Volume B: 1689–1733*
Volume C: 1732–1745	*Volume D: 1742–1756*
Volume E: 1756–1763	*Volume F: 1763–1767*
Volume G: 1767–1771	*Volume H: 1771–1782*
Volume I: 1782–1790	*Volume J: 1790–1795*
Volume K: 1795–1799	*Volume L: 1799–1801*

International Standard Book Number
Paperbound: 978-1-68034-902-3

NOTES

The figures at upper left of each abstract represent the Liber and Folio, in the original records, on which the abstracted material begins.

For the most part, each abstract includes a deed and all supporting documents (Power of Attorney, Bond, etc.) recorded with the deed.

References in the Index are to Liber and Folio in the original records, as shown at upper left of each abstract.

1 old 4/Feb 27 1669/Thomas Taylor & wf (Frances) to Arthur Wright: "Taylor's Inheritance" - 1200 a. more or less on an island, Slaughter Creek & St. John's Creek. Wit: Robt. Seale, Raymund Staplefort, Edward Hughes. Acknowledged before Edward Savuage, Clk, Mar 1 1669.

1 Old 6/Feb 28 1669/Thomas Taylor & Frances Taylor, his wife, to Robt. Seale: "Musketta Quart," 50 a. more or less on Hungar River, adj Richd. Prestone. Wit: Ar. Wright, Raymund Staplefort, Edward Hughes. Acknowledged before Edwd. Savuage, Clk, Mar 1 1669.

1 Old 8/Feb 20 1669/Richard Buttwell, Planter, to Wm Brice: "Buttwell's Choice" near the head of Little Choptank River adj lands of Robert. Winsmore - 100 a. more or less. Wit: John Dossey, Will. Dossey. Acknowledged before Edwd. Savuage, Clk, Mar 1 1669.

1 Old 9/Jan 29 1669/James Selby of Little Choptank, Planter, to Will. Merchant and James Ogg, Planters: "Selby's Desire" at head of Black Water adj land of Isaac Abrahams - 100 a. more or less. Wit: Thomas. Taylor, Will. Stevens Junr. Acknowledged before Edward Savuage, Clk, Mar 1 1669. Receipt for 2 shillings from James Ogg - Thomas Taylor, Sherriff.

1 Old 11/Mar 2 1669/John Hudson, Planter, to Bartholomew Enolds, Planter, late of the Colony of Virginia: "John's Point" on south side of Little Choptank River at Tobaccostick Creek - 200 a. Wit: James Selby, A. Wright. Acknowledged before Edward Savuage, Clk, Mar 1, 1669.

1 Old 15/Mar 1 1669/Thomas Taylor, High Sheriff, to Daniel Holland, Planter: "Taylor's Island" (2 islands) at the "Streights of Annemesick" - 220 a. more or less. Frances, wf of Thomas Taylor. Wit: A. Wright, Phillipp Shapleigh. Acknowledged before Edward Savuage, Clk, Mar 1 1669.

1 Old 17/Mar 1 1669/Thomas Taylor, High Sherr. to Daniel Holland, Planter: "St. John's Island" nr. "Streights of Annamesex" - 80 a. more or less. Frances, wf of Thomas Taylor. Wit: A. Wright, Phillip Shapleigh. Acknowledged before Edward Savuage, Mar 1 1669.

1 Old 18/Dec 2 1669/Robt. Harwood of Talbot County Planter to Edmond Brannocke, Planter: "Harwood's Choice" in Little Choptank River & South Branch of Fishing Creek. Wit: James Selby, Edwd. Savuage. Acknowledged before Edward Savuage, Clk, Jun 7 1670.

1 Old 21/Jun 7 1670/Peter Sharpe of Calvert County, Chirurgeon, to William Ticke, Planter: (Judeth, wf of Peter Sharpe) 1/2 of 250 a. called "Tenton" in Fishing Creek & Little Choptank River. Patent acknowledged before the Governor Nov 1 1665. Other Moyety or half of sd 250 a. sold to Obedh. Judkin. Wit: A. Wright, Wm Winsmore, Danl Clerke. Acknowledged before Edwd Savuage, Clk, Jun 7 1670.

1 Old 22/Nov 13 1669/Will Killman of Little Choptank, Planter, to Robt Lambden, Planter: Part of "Armstrong's Folly," 200 a. more or less on Little Choptank and Chesapeake Bay. Judeth, wf of Will Killman. Acknowledged before Edward Savuage, Clk, Jun 7 1670.

1 Old 24/Aug 2 1670/Thomas Hooton, Planter, to Isaac Hunt, Planter: "Hooton's Neck" on Chesapeake Bay & Hungar River. Wit: Thos Skinner, James Selby. Acknowledged before Edwd Sauvage, Clk, Aug 2 1670

1 Old 26/Jan 30 1669/Wm Southbee (Southby) of Miles River, Talbot County, Planter, to Nicholas Mace of Fishing Creek Hundred in Little Choptank River, Planter: Land on Little Choptank River & Fishing Creek, purchased by Southby

from John Gary of the Clifts in Calvert County, containing 200 a. Wit:
Thomas Wall, John Faucett. Steven Gary, Atty to Will Southby. Acknowledged
before Edwd Sauvage, Clk, Aug 2 1670.

1 Old 29/Jun 10 1670/John Brookes of Dorchester County, Chirurgeon, to John
Avery, "Boat Write" of afsd County: " a little neck of land in the bay behind
St. Jameses point on the Eastn. Shore." Wit: Daniell Clercke, John Pollard.
Acknowledged before Edwd Sauvage, Clk, Aug 2 1670.

1 Old 31/Aug 2 1670/Robert Lambden, Planter, to Richard Gibbs of Worcestershire, England, Merchant: Part of "Armstrong's Folly," 200 a. on James'
Island. Mary, wf of Robt Lambden. Wit: Peter Baucomb, John Avery. Acknowledged before Edwd Sauvage, Clk, Aug 2 1670. Power of Atty from Peter Sharpe,
Atty for Richard Gibbs, to John Gary, son in law of sd Peter Sharpe.

1 Old 33/Mar 1 1669/Isaac Abram of Talbot County, Planter, to Peter Sharpe of
Calvert County, Chirurgeon: Land on Little Choptank River and Back Creek,
called "Marsh Land." 150 a. more or less. Elizabeth, wf of Isaac Abram.
Wit: A. Wright, Edwd Sauvage. Acknowledged before Edwd Sauvage, Clk, Sep
6 1670.

1 Old 35/Sep 6 1670/John Edmondson of Talbot County and Sarah his wife to
John Webster: "Edmondson's Desire" on Edmondson's Creek on South side of
Choptank River. Wit: Anthony Dawson, John Standley. Acknowledged before
Edwd Sauvage, Clr, Sep 6 1670.

1 Old 36/John Everard of Talbot County, Planter, to John Edmondson: 150 a.,
part of a parcel of land laid out by George Richardson for Robert Harwood on
Little Choptank River & Fishing Creek, originally 300 a. Wit: Will. Kircome,
John Stanley. Acknowledged by Peter Baucombe, Atty for John Everard, before
Edwd Sauvage, Clk, Sep 6 1670.

1 Old 38/Sep 6 1670/John Edmondson of Talbot County and Sarah his wf to
Cuthbert Phillips: "York," containing 300 a. by estimation, in Talbot County,
adj John Smith's land. Wit: John Webster, John Stanley. Acknowledged before
Edwd Sauvage, Clk, Sep 6 1670. Peter Baucombe, Atty for Cuthbert Phillips of
Talbot County. Power of Atty witnessed by Will. Watson and John Stanley.

1 Old 39/Feb 18 1668/John Edmondson and Sarah his wf of Talbot County to
Bartholomew Ennalls: "In consideration of a Sloope called the Endavour of a
burthen about forty Hodgsheads already Recd. and a Bill of Ten thousand
pounds of Tobo. in Caske," parcel of land called "St. Johns Purchase" lying
in Transquaking River in Talbot County in the North Branch of the River.
Two(?) thousand a. more or less. Wit: Thomas Skillington, Joseph Lane.
Acknowledged in Talbot County Court before Wm Henesley(?), Clk, Feb 16 1668.
Acknowledged before Edwd Sauvage, Clk, Sep 6 1670.

1 Old 40/Oct 28 1669/John Hudson to Anthony Tall: Part (1/3) of "Hudson's
Desire" granted to John Hudson by Lord Baltimore Apr 1 1668. 150 a. in
original grant; 50 a. conveyed to Tall. Wit: Daniell Clarke, Edwd Sauvage.
Acknowledged before Edward Sauvage, Clk, Nov 1 1670.

1 Old 44/Nov 1 1670/Thomas Oliver and Lawrance Simmons of Talbot County to
William Killman of Jameses Island, Dorchester County: "Long Point" on James
Island adj land laid out for Frances Armstrong late of the sd province called
"Armstrong's Hogg Penn." By estimation 200 a. Wit: Peter Baucombe, Edward
Sauvage. Acknowledged before Edward Sauvage, Clk, Nov 1 1670. Peter
Baucombe, Atty for Lawrance Simmons. Seath Simmons, wf of Lawrance Simmons.
Power of Atty witnessed by John Scott and Samuel Crickhils(?).

1 Old 46/Patent to Francis Armstong for 350 a. called "Sarke" bearing date at
St. Mary's the eighth day of March 1663, with the 3 following assignments:
Francis Armstrong and Frances his wf to John Edmondson, Mar 24 1663. Wit:
A. Skinner, Thos Manning. John Edmondson to Peter Baucombe, Jun 4 1666. Wit:
James Shacklady, Thomas Goddard. Peter Baucombe to John Edmondson, Nov 2
1670. Acknowldeged by John Edmondson to Henry Trippe before Edward Sauvage,
Clk, Nov 2 1670.

1 Old 47/Patent to John Edmondson for 200 a. called "Nuncock" (or "Nimcock")
dated at St. Mary's Jun 27 1664, with the following assignments: John Edmondson to Peter Baucomb, Jun 4 1670. Wit: James Shacklady, Thomas Goddard.
Peter Baucomb to John Edmondson, Nov 2 1670. Acknowledged by John Edmondson
to Henry Tripp before Edward Sauvage, Clk, Nov 2 1670.

1 Old 47/Nov 2 1670/Agreement by Henry Tripp re line between "Sarke" and the
land of Jos Lane adj thereto, known as "Gotam(?.)." Wit: Thomas Taylor, Will.
Fowler. Acknowledged before Edwd Sauvage, Clk, Nov 2 1670.

1 Old 48/Bond from John Edmondson of Talbot County, Merchant, to Henry Tripp
of Little Choptank River, Dorchester County, Gentleman. Sarah, wf of John
Edmondson. Wit: Thomas Taylor, Wm Fowler, Wm Travice.

1 Old 50/Nov 2 1670/John Edmondson to Henry Tripp, 350 a. known as "Sarke" on
Armstrong's Bay, patented to Francis Armstrong Mar 8 1663 and conveyed by
Armstrong to John Edmondson. Wit: Thomas Taylor, Wm Fowler, Wm Travice.
Acknowledged before Edward Sauvage, Clk, Nov 2 1670.

1 Old 52/Nov 2 1670/John Edmondson to Henry Tripp, 200 a. called "Nimcock"
patented to Edmondson Jun 27 1664, on the south side of Choptank in a bay
called Armstrong's Bay, adj land laid out for Francis Armstrong, called
"Sarke." Wit: Thomas Taylor, Wm Fowler, Wm Travice.

1 Old 54/Sep 16 1670/James Selby To Edmond Brannock: "Brannock's Adventure,"
50 a. more or less on Fishing Creek in Little Choptank River, adj lands of
Peter Sharp and John Gather. Acknowledged before Edward Sauvage, Clk, Jun
18 1670.

1 Old 55/Jan 17 1670/Henry Aldredge, Cooper, to John Brooke, Chirurgeon: 50
a. on Hudson's Creek. Wit: Edward Cooke, Mathias Woods. Acknowledged before
Edward Sauvage, Clk, Jan 17 1670.

1 Old 56/Dec 2 1670/Daniel Payne of Northhampton County, Virginia, Planter,
to Thomas Kendall of the same County, Power of Atty. Wit: Edward Ashby, Owen
Narshy. Receipt from Thomas Kendall, Atty for Daniel Payne, to John Robert-
son for debts due John McKeele, Adam Thoroughgood, Kendall or Payne. Wit:
A. Wright, Hen. Beckwith, Mathias Woods.

1 Old 57/Apr 1 1670/Assignment of Deed from Wm Killman and Judeth his wf to
Robert Lambden. Robert Lambden and wf, Mary O. Lambden, to Richard Gibbs of
Worcester, England, Merchant. Wit: Thos Galpen, John Webster. Peter Sharpe,
Atty for Richard Gibbs. Acknowledged before Edwd Sauvage, Clk, Jun 7 1670.

1 Old 57/Power of Atty from Wm Killman of James Island, to James Selby, to
receive a deed for 200 a. called "Long Point" on James Island from Lawrence
Simmons and Thomas Oliver. Wit: Thomas Pattison, Jacob Jenifer.

1 Old 58/Aug 3 1670/Bond from Thomas Hooton to Isaac Hunt re 50 a. of land
sold by sd Thomas Hooton to said Isaac Hunt. Receipt of A. Wright, Sub. :
Sherr., for one shilling from Thomas Hooton for alienation of 50 a. of land
called Hooton's Neck.

1 Old 59/Mar 9 1668/Jefory Summerford of Dorchester County, Lawyer and Admr. of the Estate of John Six, deceased, and Siball his wife, formerly the relict of sd John Six, to Cornelius Watkinson of Calvert County, Carpenter: Land in Calvert County granted to John Six by Lord Baltimore by patent dated Nov 25 1667. Acknowledged in Open Court by Jefory Summerford and Siball his wife, Mar 9 1668-9, before Raymond Staplefort and John Felton, Gent.

1 Old 61/Aug 2 1669/Daniel Clarke of Little Choptank, Gent. to William Merchant, planter and Henry Turner, Carpenter: "Clarke's Outlett" on Salt Marsh Creek and Clark's Marsh in Little Choptank River, 100 a. more or less. Wit: James Selby, Morrice Mathews. Power of Atty witnessed by James Selby and Stephen Zealous. Acknowledged in Open Court before Commissioners by Edward Sauvage, Atty for Daniel Clarke, Aug 3 1669.

1 Old 64/Sep 6 1669/John Hodson, Planter to John Mackeele, Planter: Part of "Hodson's Desire" on Tobacco Stick Bay patented to Hodson Apr 1 1668. Originally 150 a.; 100 a. conveyed to Mackeele. Wit: Phillip Shapleigh, Edward Sauvage. Acknowledged in Open Court Sep 7 1669. Edward Sauvage, Clk.

1 Old 68/Feb 6 1665/John Pitt of Isle of White County, Virginia to John Alford of Little Choptank: "Musketta Quarter" on Tobacco Stick Creek, 200 a. more or less. Wit: Richard Howard, Samuell Prichard, Thomas Skinner. John Hodson, Atty to John Pitt. Acknowledged Sep 7 1669 in Open Court. Edward Sauvage, Clk. Receipt from Charles Calvert for 4 shillings paid by Daniel Clarke, Atty for John Pitt, for Alienation of 200 a.

1 Old 70/Oct 9 1669/Bond of Stephen Gary to James Modesley re 100 a. of land in Slaughter Creek, "Ceader Point." Wit: John Pollard, William Stephens, Henry Hooper.

1 Old 71/Power Atty from Judeth Killman to Thomas Brown, to acknowledge to Robert Lambden 200 a. of land called "Armstrong's Folly" sold to Lambden by the husband of Judeth Killman. Wit: Raymond Staplefort, William Jones.

1 Old 71/Apr 11 1664/Thomas Manning of the Clifts in Calvert County, Planter, and Grace Manning his wf to Andrew Cooke of London, England, Merchant: 200 a. patented Sep 9 1663, called "Papae Thickett" in Fishing Creek and Little Choptank River. Wit: James Elton, ___ Ingram. Daniel Clarke, Atty for Thomas Manning and Grace his wf; Power of Atty witnessed by Morrice Mathews and Richard Butwell. Acknowledged in open Court Nov 2 1669 - Edward Sauvage, Clk.

1 Old 72/Sep 17 1668/Andrew Cooke of London to Thomas Newton: 200 a. called "Papae Thickett" on Little Choptank River and Fishing Creek. Patented Sep 9 1663. Wit: Thos Manning, Daniel Clarke. Acknowledged Nov 2 1669 by Daniel Clarke, Atty for Andrew Cooke - Edward Sauvage, Clk.

1 Old 74/Peter Sharpe and Judeth his wife to Edward Taylor and Nicholas Mace: Assignment of patent for 150 a. called "Fishing Creek." Patent dated Jul 28 1664. Wit: John Barber, Symon Clymor, Franc. Taylor. Acknowledged Nov 21 1665 before Charles Calvert.

1 Old 75/Oct 28 1669/Nicholas Mace to William Hill: 75 a. of "Fishing Creek" patented to Peter Sharpe Jul 28 1664 and assigned to Edward Taylor and Nicholas Mace. Wit: Henry Trippe, Edward Sauvage. Acknowledged in Open Court Nov 2 1669. Edward Sauvage, Clk.

1 Old 79/Oct 28 1669/Richard Webb of Calvert County, Planter to Thomas Wall of Dorchester County, Planter: 100 a. called "Snake Point" on the west side

of Fishing Creek patented to Webb Aug 20 1668. Wit: Daniel Clarke, Edward Sauvage. Acknowledged in Open Court Nov 2 1669. Edward Sauvage, Clk.

1 Old 83/Nov 9 1669/Robert Hayle of Talbot County, Planter, to Anthony Hardacre of Dorchester County, Planter: "Hayle's Chorce" on Little Choptank River and Fishing Creek, 100 a. Wit: Thomas Wall, Henry Aldred. Acknowledged in Open Court Jan 4 1669 by Stephen Gary, Atty for Robert Hayle. Edward Sauvage, Clk. Power of Atty witnessed by Henry Aldred and Edmond Brannock. Receipt from Arthur Wright, Sub. Sherr. for 2 shillings pd. by Stephen Gary for alienation of 100 a. called "Hayle's Choyce."

1 Old 86/Jul 8 1669/William Travers to Robert Gould: 150 a. near Broad Marsh on Nanticoke River. Wit: John Beard, Thomas James. Acknowledged Sep 6 1670 before Edward Sauvage, Clk.

1 Old 88/Jul 20 1668/Timothy Goodridge to William Travers and Nicholas Hackett: Land on Nanticoke River near Broad Marsh, 300 a. more or less. Wit: Fran. Armstrong, William Young. The one moyety of 150 a. in this parcel of land was acknowledged by William Travers to Nicholas Hackett Sep 6 1670. Edward Sauvage, Clk.

1 Old 89/Sep 6 1670/John Edmondson and Sarah his wf to Richard Holland, Millwright: "Doncaster" on Edmondson's Neck. Wit: Anthony Dawson, John Standley. Acknowledged before Edward Sauvage, Clk. - Sep 6 1670. Bond witnessed by Peter Baucomb, John Standley.

1 Old 91/Sep 30 1670/John Edmondson to Daniel Jones: One Moyety of "Harwood's Desire," 150 a. which is the uppermost part of the said land, on Little Choptank River & Fishing Creek. Wit: Peter Baucomb, Edward Cooke. Acknowledged Nov 1 1670. Edward Sauvage, Clk.

1 Old 92/Sep 30 1670/Daniel Jones to John Edmondson: "Fox Hill," 200 a. on south side of Choptank. Wit: Peter Baucombe, Edward Cooke. Acknowledged Nov 1 1670. Edward Sauvage, Clk.

1 Old 93/Feb 22 1671/John Kirke to Francis Tassell: 1/3 of parcel of land estimated at 200 a. called "Ricarton," on south side of Great Choptank at Hughs Creek, purchased by Kirk from Daniel Jones according to bill of sale dated Oct 3 1668. Wit: Benjamin Wood, Thomas Roberts.

1 Old 94/Oct 6 1670/Robert Harwood of Miles River, Talbot County, to William Worgin of Fishing Creek: 150 a., 1/2 of "Harwood's Choice," a tract of land on Fishing Creek and Little Choptank River adj land formerly laid out for Stephen Gary. Alice, wife of Wm Worgin. Wit: Anthony Dawson, Stephen Gary. Acknowledged Mar 7 1670. Edward Sauvage, Clk.

1 Old 97/Feb 6 1670/Raymond Staplefort of Hungar River to William Broughton (Wroughton): 100 a. called "Staplefort's Lott" on the N.E. side of Hungar River. Wit: Thos Taylor, Arthur Wright. Acknowldeged by Raymond Staplefort and Eleanor his wife, Mar 7 1670. Edward Sauvage, Clk.

1 Old 101/Nov 6 1688/Samuel Millington and Ruth his wife to Samuel Harper, Godson of Samuel Millington: 50 a. called "Hooton's Neck" on Hungar River. Wit: Benjamin Hunt, Thos Pattison. Acknowledged Nov 6 1688 before Thos Taylor and Jno Woodward. Thos Pattison, Clk.

1 Old 101/Aug 20 1688/Charles Hutchins of Dorchester County, planter, and Ann, his wife, to William Smith: "Smithfield" on the East side of Chicanomico River, 400 a. more or less, granted to Hutchins by patent dated May 30 1683. Wit: Jno Booth, Wm Harrison. Acknowledged Aug 20 1688 before Thos Taylor and

Jno Hodson.   Thomas Pattison, Clk.

1 Old 102/Aug 6 1688/John Spicer to John Norman: Part of "Collchester" con-
taining 340 a. more or less patented to John Spicer, adj land of Hannah
Hungerford and John Norman. 50 a. conveyed. Norah, wife of John Spicer.
Wit: Phill. Pitt, Thos Pattison. Acknowledged by John Spicer and Norah his
wife and Elizabeth Winged, Aug 6 1689, before Jacob Loockerman and John
Woodward. Thos Pattison, Clk.

1 Old 104/Aug 7 1689/William Dossey of Dorchester County, planter, and Mary
his wife, to Thomas Ennalls, Mariner, of Dorchester County: "Dossey's Choice"
on Chicanocomoco River, ajd "Causes Lott" and land formerly laid out for
Thomas Smithson, Bartholomew Ennalls and William Dolebury and the land of
Adam Moxson. 130 a. more or less. Wit: Benj Hunt, John Newton. Acknowledged Aug 7 1689 before John Brooke and John Woodward. Thos Pattison, Clk.
"Received of Mr. Thos. Ennalls, by order of Mr. Edward Pindar High Sheriff
the sum of five shilling sixpence for alienation of the withinmentioned land.
Aug. ye 7th 1689   Pr me Wm. Hill   Sub. Sheriff"

1 Old 106/Jan 14 1687-8/William Dorrington to John Edmondson, William Sharpe
and John Stephens (Trustees): For the natural love, good will and affection
of William Dorrington for William Dorrington and Ann Dorrington, his children, issue of his deceased wife Elizabeth Dorrington, alias Winsloe; and
William Winsloe, brother in law of William Dorrington, land on Jenkins Creek
and Great Choptank River. Lot called "Busby" containing 500 a.; "Temple
Street" containing 200 a.;"Hoggs Hole" containing 100 a.; "Clift" containing
200 a.; "Clifton" containing 200 a. - 1275 a. in all. Life estates to children and brother in law with remainder, if life tenants leave no issue, to
Quakers. Sarah Dorrington, alias Fisher, daughter of William Dorrington.
Wit: John Mallington, Henry Howard, Ann Glassington, Daniel Smith, Arthur
Whiteley, Maurice Mathews. Acknowledged Feb 8 1689 in open Court - Samuel
Cmith, Clk. Deed voided Aug 6 1689 by Phill. Pitt, Atty for William Dorring-
ton. Thos Pattison, Clk.

1 Old 108/Jan 4 1689/Thomas Pattison and Ann his wife to Thomas Wells, Millwright: "Charleston" on Cabin Creek near Secretary Creek, 200 a. more or
less. Wit: Franc. Twyford, Daniel Lawrence. Thomas Cooke, Atty for Ann
Pattison. Acknowledged in Open Court Jan 7 1689/90. Thos Pattison, Clk.

1 Old 110/May 13 1690/John Gooty Sr and Margaret his wife to John Gooty Jr:
"Insley's Point" on Transquakin River, 50 a. purchased by John Gooty Sr from
Andrew Insley (deed Jan 8 1678); "Bowbunck" on Blackwater River near
"Margaret Point," 100 a. patented to John Gooty Sr Jul 19 1681; "Callie" on
Blackwater River, 250 a. adj land formerly belonging to Andrew Insley,
patented to John Gooty Sr Jul 22 1681. Wit: Michael Todd, Jacob Jenifer.
Thomas Cooke, Atty for Margaret Gooty. Acknowledged before Charles Huchins
and Jacob Loockerman, Jun 5 1690. Thos Pattison, Clk.

1 Old 112/mar 1 1690/Thomas Wall to John Young, Weaver: "Wallborough" on
Transquakin River, 59 a. more or less. Acknowledged Mar 4 1690. Thos
Pattison, Clk.

1 Old 113/Feb 17 1690/Thomas Norcombe and Mary his wife to John Davis: 1/2 of
"the Plaines," estimated at 300 a. on Hunting Creek in Great Choptank River.
Wit: Thomas Colton, Anthony Squires. Acknowledged Mar 3 1690/1. Thos
Pattison, Clk.

1 Old 114/Jul 30 1690/Daniel Clarke to Edward Cooke: In consideration of the
formation of a partnership between Clarke and Cooke, 1/3 of Clarke's estate

-6-

at death to go to Cooke. Edward Cooke the Younger, mentioned as the son of Edward Cooke. If Edward Cooke, Sr, predeceases Kath. Kennedy of Dorchester County, the 1/3 of Clarke's estate to go to said Katherine Kennedy. Wit: Phill. Pitt, Wm Sanders. Recorded Aug 20 1690. Thos Pattison, Clk.

1 Old 116/May 1 1690/Henry Griffith and Elizabeth his wife to John Welch: "Wattson's Lott" on Hunting Creek on south side of Great Choptank River. 100 a. more or less. Wit: Gournay Crowe, Andrew Parker, John Kirke. Acknowledged Aug 8 1690. Thos Pattison, Clk.

1 Old 118/Aug 7 1690/John Ross and Mable his wife to Thomas Phillips: 58 a., part of a tract patented to Ross Aug 20 1683 containing 200 a. more or less between Hodson's Creek and Arthur Wright's Creek. Wit: Arthur Whiteley, John Draper, Thomas Pattison. Acknowledged Aug 7 1690 before John Hodson and John Mackeel, Sr, Justices. Thos: Pattison, Clk.

1 Old 120/Sep 1 1690/Capt. Thomas Ennalls, Mariner, and Elizabeth his wife to Francis Hayward, Planter: "Francis Cottage" on Transquakin River. 200 a. more or less. Acknowledged in open court Sep 2 1690. Thos Pattison, Clk.

1 Old 121/1690/John Rawlings to Benjamin Hunt: "Inheritance" on Blackwater River, 300 a. more or less. Acknowledged Sep 2 1690 before John Brooke and Thos Hicks. Thos Pattison, Clk.

1 Old 122/1690/Benjamin Hunt to John Rawlings: "Bedminster" on Transquakin River adj "Taylor's Delight" and adj Henry Turner's "Quinborough" 150 a. more or less. Acknowledged Sep 2 1690 before John Brooke and Thomas Hicks. Thos Pattison, Clk.

1 Old 123/Nov 12 1688/Thomas Wall to Thomas Ennalls: 1/2 of "Worgan's Chance" formerly purchased from Thomas Taylor by Edward Sauvage, laid out for 25 a. Also a parcel of land on Fishing Creek laid out for 50 a. (75 a. in all). Also 50 a. of "Worgan's Chance." Also 50 a., "Worgan's Adventure" on Little Choptank River and Fishing Creek adj land of Robert Harwood. Wit: Phill. Pitt, Hugh Eccleston, Thomas Hicks. Acknowledged Nov 14 1688 before Thomas Taylor, Jacob Loockerman. Receipt for 3 shillings and sixpence for alienation of land. Edward Pinder, Sheriff. Thomas Pattison, Clk.

1 Old 124/Oct 25 1690/Thomas Pattison and Ann his wife to their daughter Elizabeth Pattison: "Paden Arme" in Taylor's Island adj Purnell's Land on the Eastern side of Purnell's Cove, 81 a. more or less, patented to Thomas Pattison Jun 1 1685. Wit: John Keene, John Robson. Acknowledged in open court. Thomas Pattison, Clk.

1 Old 125/Nov 6 1690/Thomas Oliver to Humphrey Hubbart: "Refuge" on west side of Transquakin River, 50 a. more or less adj "Strawberry Garden." Wit: James Benson, Wm Dossey, Franc. Anderton. Acknow. Nov 5 1690 in open court. Thos Pattison, Clk.

1 Old 126/Nov 5 1690/John Foster and Mary his wife to William Stephens, William Kennerly and Edward Fisher for themselves and on behalf of the Quakers: "One dwelling house for a meetinghouse with one acre of ground whereon the said meeting house standeth," part of 200 a. called "Exchange" formerly bought of Thomas Pattison of Oyster Creek. Wit: John Brookes, John Hazlewood. Acknowledged in open Court. Thomas Pattison, Clk.

1 Old 127/William Stephens to Jane Stephens, his wife: Dwelling plantation on Transquakin River for her natural life, and 1/3 of his Moveables after his decease. Wit: John Brookes, William Powell. Acknowledged in open court Nov 5 1690. Thos Pattison, Clk.

1 Old 127/Jul 10 1690/John Edmondson and Sarah his wife to John Nichols:
"Richeson's Choyce," 532 a. between Marsh Creek and Hunting Creek, adj "Fox
Hill" and "Skipton." Wit: Arthur Knowles, John Tisdell. Acknowledged Nov
4 1690 before John Brooke, Charles Huchins. Thos Pattison, Clk.

1 Old 129/Jul 1 1690/John Edmondson and Sarah his wife to John Wade: 1/2 of
the "Range" on Marsh Creek adj "Richeson's Folly and "Skipton." Original
lot 400 a.; 200 a. conveyed. Wit: John Stanley, John Nicholls. Acknowledged
Nov 4 1690 before John Brooke, Chas Huchins. Thos Pattison, Clk.

1 Old 130/Jan 6 1690/John Taylor to John Kirke: "Grove" on the East side of
N.W. Fork of Nanticoke. 300 a. more or less adj land of John Pierce. Wit:
Thos Cooke, Franc. Anderton. Acknowledged in open court by Thomas Cooke,
Atty for John Taylor. Thomas Pattison, Clk. Letter of Atty witnessed by
Edward Pindar, Franc. Anderton.

1 Old 131/Mar 4 1691/Thomas Killman, Planter to Thomas Pattison, Wine Cooper:
1/2 of land formerly laid out for Francis Armstrong called "Armstrong's
Folly" on James Island. Originally 400 a.; 200 a. conveyed. Acknowledged
Mar 4 1690/91. Thos Pattison, Clk.

1 Old 132/May 12 1686/George Ferguson to Joseph Stanaway: "Ferguson's Forrest"
in Hungar River containing 150 a. more or less. Wit: Edward Bentall, William
Goodine. Acknowledged Mar 3 1690. Thos Pattison, Clk.

1 Old 134/Mar 4 1691/Thomas Taylor and Frances his wife to Thomas Killman:
"Whinfield Trouble," 200 a. more or less. Acknowledged Mar 4 1690/91. Thos
Pattison, Clk.

1 Old 135/Jun 1 1691/John Jones and William Jones and Jennett his wife to
Richard Tubman: "George Point" on Slaughter Creek and Newton's Marsh, 100 a.
more or less patented to Thomas Newton Aug 31 1670.
Also "His Excellency's Grant to Jones" in Hungar River, 50 a. more or less.
Also "Jones Orchard" on Hungar River adj "His Excellency's Grant to Jones,"
4 a. more or less. Also "Jones' Chance" on Hungar River adj "His Excellency's
Grant to Jones" and "Mathews Wineyard," all formerly surveyed and laid out
for William Jones late of Dorchester County, deceased. Jane Kimball, mother
of grantors, dower interest. Wit: Thomas Pattison, William Hill. Acknowledged Jun 4 1691. Thos Pattison, Clk.

1 Old 137/Jun 2 1691/Thomas Pattison and Ann his wife to Richard Adams:
"Buckland" on Secretary Creek, 150 a. more or less, patented to said Thomas
Pattison Sep 10 1683, except 100 a. called "Westward" granted to Edward
Taylor Jr. Acknowledged Jun 2 1691. Thos Pattison, Clk.

1 Old 139/Feb 3 1691/William Brice to John Leighy: Land in Cabin Creek, 100 a.
more or less, called "Whitlewood." Wit: Phill. Pitt, Hen. Whitaker. Acknowledged in open court by Thomas Wells, Atty for William Brice, Mar 3 1690/91.
Thomas Pattison, Clk.

1 Old 140/Jun 2 1691/Thomas Wells to William Spencer: 100 a., moyety of 200
a. purchased from Thomas Pattison on Cabin Creek and Secretary Creek, called
"Charleton." Wit: Phill. Pitt, Hen. Whitaker. Margaret Wells, wife of
Thomas Wells. Acknowledged Jun 2 1691. Thos Pattison, Clk.

1 Old 141/Jun 2 1691/Thomas Wells to William Lowe: 100 a. of "Charleston"
purchased from Thomas Pattison. Wit: Phill. Pitt, Hen. Whitaker. Margaret
Wells, wife of Thomas Wells. Acknowledged Jun 2 1690/91. Thos Pattison,
Clk.

1 Old 142/Nov 20 1690/John Meredith to William Wraughton: "Vale of Misery" between Blackwater and Hungar Rivers on the East side of Transquakin Creek. 100 a. Wit: Edwd Bentall, John Pottenger. Acknowledged by John Meredith and Sarah his wife, Jun 2 1691. Thos Pattison, Clk.

1 Old 143/Sep 1 1690/William Buckley to John Dowdall: "Parthomall" adj land of John Briggs, 50 a. more or less on South side of Choptank River. Wit: Phill. Pitt, John Richards. Acknowledged Jan 6 1690/91. Thos Pattison, Clk.

1 Old 145/May 21 1690/Cornelius Mullraigne to Richard Foster: "Mullraigne," 150 a. on Great Choptank River & Tuckaho, near land of Wm Berry. Wit: John Sleharty, Robert Carney, John Dondall. Mary Mullraigne, wife of Cornelius Mullraigne. Acknowledged Aug 1691. Thos Pattison, Clk.

1 Old 146/Aug 2 1691/Elizabeth Underwood and Judith Underwood, daughters of Peter Underwood, deceased, to John Harwood: In consideration of 100 acres of land in Talbot County sold by Harwood to Elizabeth Underwood and Judith Underwood, they convey to him 50 a., 1/2 or moyety of "Castlehaven" in Dorchester County. Wit: Joseph James, Richard Moore, Simon Cuper. Acknowledged Aug 2 1691 before Henry Trippe and John Mackeel Sr. Thos Pattison, Clk.

1 Old 147/Jun 7 1683/Thomas Taylor to William Hill: "Richardson's Purchase" on Transquakin River, 500 a., except tract formerly sold to William Traverse containing 30 a. more or less. Wit: Hugh Ecclestone, John Tench. Frances, wife of Thomas Taylor. Acknowledged by Maj. Thomas Taylor Dec 14 1691 before Henry Trippe, John Brooke, Edward Pindar, Thomas Ennalls. Hugh Ecclestone, Clk.

1 Old 148/Dec 6 1686/7/Major Thomas Taylor Stewart of Dorchester County on behalf of said County from Capt. Anthony Dawson: In consideration of 26,000 pounds of Tobacco to be paid to said Dawson for erecting and building a Court-house in Cambridge, 325 a., part of a tract purchased by Dawson from Thomas Walker, called "Alexander's Place" on Transquakin River; also a dwelling house in Cambridge occupied by Mr. Thomas Cooke. (See original Deed Record for specifications for Court House). Wit: Thos Cooke, Hen. Raddon. Rebecca Dawson, wife of Anthony Dawson. Acknowledged by Rebecca Dawson Jan 1 1691/2 before John Brooke and Thos Ennalls. Wit: Phill. Pitt, Obadh. King.

1 Old 150/Nov 3 1691/John Prout to John Bramble: "Waxford" on West side of Goose Creek issuing out of Fishing Bay, containing 50 a.; also "Steeple Bumstead" near the head of Goose Creek issuing out of Fishing Bay adj "Wax-ford," containing 50 a.; also "Haverill" on Goose Creek adj "Black Valley," "Waxford," "Steeple Bumstead" and "Doe Park" containing 50 a. Wit: Thomas Pattison, Robert Pope. Katherine Prout, wife of John Prout. Acknowledged Nov 4 1691. Hugh Ecclestone, Clk.

1 Old 152/Nov 4 1691/John Boone to William Vaughan: Part of "Exchange," 150 a. Wit: John Lord, John Price. Acknowledged Nov 4 1691. Hugh Ecclestone, Clk.

1 Old 153/Mar 2 1691/Thomas Taylor and Frances his wife to Robert Mansell (or Manvell) of the Island of Barbadoes, Mariner: 1000 a. called "Jordaine Point," 100 a. called "Taylor's Outhold," 50 a. called "Piney Point," and 200 a. called "Tenches Hoope." Wit: Thos Cooke, R. Goldsborough. Acknowledged Mar 3 1691/2. Hugh Ecclestone, Clk.

1 Old 155/Feb 8 1691/Daniel Clark to Walter Campbell: "Sharpes Point" containing 200 a. on Little Choptank, for the term of the natural life of Katherine Clark, wife of Daniell Clark. Wit: Hugh Ecclestone, Phill. Pitt.

-9-

Acknowledged Feb 8 1691/2 before John Brooke and John Mackeel. Hugh Ecclestone, Clk.

1 Old 156/Nov 30 1691/John Lahey to Henry Whitaker: "Whittlewood" near Cabin Creek, containing 100 a. Wit: Hugh Ecclestone, William Gray. Acknowledged Mar 1 1691/2. Hugh Ecclestone, Clk.

1 Old 158/Feb 29 1691/2/William Low and Sarah his wife to Andrew Gray: 100 a. of "Charleton," originally 200 a., near Cabin Creek. Wit: John Hazlewood, Richard Owen. Acknowledged Mar 1 1691/2 by William Low and Phill. Pitt, Atty for Sarah Low. Hugh Ecclestone, Clk. Letter of Atty of Sarah Low refers to Gray as "Andrew Gray junr."

1 Old 160/1691/Maj. Thomas Taylor and Frances his wife to John Branock: 250 a. more or less between Jordan's Point and Manning's Point on Chesapeake Bay, adj land of Thomas Jordan. Wit: Andrew Parker, Thos Cooke, R. Goldsborough. Acknowledged Mar 3 1691/2. Hugh Ecclestone, Clk.

1 Old 161/1691/Maj. Thomas Taylor and Frances his wife to John Branock: "Tripp's Ridge" at the head of Tripp's Creek, on Little Choptank River adj land formerly laid out for Michael Brooke; 150 a. more or less. Wit: Andrew Parker, Thos Cooke, R. Goldsborough. Acknowledged Mar 3 1691/2. Hugh Ecclestone, Clk.

1 Old 162/Mar 1 1692/Thomas Wall to John Young: "Thames Street," 100 a. more or less laid out for said Thomas Wall. Wit: Thomas Ennalls, John Kirk. Acknowledged Mar 2 1691/2. Hugh Ecclestone, Clk.

1 Old 164/Mar 1 1692/John Young to James Peterkin: Land in Transquakin River called "Walborough" containing 59 a. more or less. Wit: John Kirk, Thomas Wall. Acknowledged Mar 2 1691/2. Hugh Ecclestone, Clk.

1 Old 165/Jul 31 1686/William Berry to Richard Foster: "Berry's Point" containing 50 a. more or less. Wit: Nicholas Wayman, William Stephens. "Edward Pinder   April 26th, 1692
    Kind Uncle being at present indisposed in body yt I know not when I can come into ye County or to ye Court & Richard Foster desiring me to acknowledge his deed wch. my father decd. in his Life time did make Seal and Deliver, I have made bould to Nomitiate thee to deliver ye said deed in Court before Two or more Justices as by ye above L. of Attorney appears wch Act of Kindness I doe Desire of thee and for Retaliation I Desire thee to make Use of me in any thing that I am Cabable of & Shall readily do my utmost ye with due respects to they self and Aunt I rest thy Loveing Kindsman Wm. Berry" Letter of Attorney from William Berry, son and Administrator of William Berry deceased, to Edward Pinder to acknowledge to Richard Foster 50 a. called "Berry's Range" sold by said Wm. Berry deceased. Witnessed by Hinrich Gansen, Naomy Perry. Acknowledged by Edward Pinder Apr 28 1692. Hugh Ecclestone, Clk.

1 Old 167/Jun 15 1688/Letter of Attorney from Thomas Smithson of Dorchester County to William Hill. Wit: Hugh Ecclestone, Richd. Addams. Proved by oath of Hugh Ecclestone, before Dr. John Brook and Mr. Edward Pinder, Justices, Jan 5 1691/2. Hugh Ecclestone, Clk.

1 Old 167/Dec 11 1678/

	(Daniell Clark)		(Henry Tripp)	
Prest:	(Robt. Winsmore)	of ye Quo.	( )	) Justices
	(Wm. Stevens)		(Thos. Skinner)	

Testimony of John Edmondson re bounds of land of John Horn of Horn's Point marked by William Coursey, Surveyor, and John Edmondson. Wit: Robert Winsmore, Thomas Taylor.

1 Old 168/Oct 6 1674/William Worgin to Justices of Dorchester County: 25 a. of "Harwood's Choice" with a house lately built be George Seward, for use as a Court House as long as it is used as such; to be returned to Worgin when no longer used by the Court. Edward Sauvage, Clk.

1 Old 168/Nov 13 1674/John Richardson to Edward Cook: Part of "Fox Hill" in Marshy Creek. Wit: George Roe, Susan Richardson. Acknowledged Dec 1 1674. Edward Sauvage, Clk.

1 Old 169/Feb 29 1674/Miles Mason and Ann his wife to John Rawlings: Land called "Mason's Yard" containing 150 a. more or less. Wit: Anthony Dawson, Thomas Vicars. Acknowledged the 2nd Tuesday in June, 1675. Edward Sauvage, Clk.

1 Old 171/Francis Twyford to William Jones: Power Atty re land called "George's Choice" sold to Twyford by Thomas Newton. Wit: Gourney Crowe, Thomas Vicars. Acknowledged Jun 2 1675. Edward Sauvage, Clk.

1 Old 172/Jun 23 1675/John Rowland to William Wroughton: Gift of all his property. Wit: John Phillips, John Miller, W. Browne, John Pippell. Acknowledged Sep 7 1675. Edward Sauvage, Clk.

1 Old 173/Jun 20 1675/John Rowland to William Wroughton: Power of Atty. Wit: John Phillips, John Miller, Wm Browne, John Sippell. Acknowledged Sep 7 1675. Edward Sauvage, Clk.

1 Old 174/Oct 29 1674/Thomas Phillips to William Simpson: Land called "Grovelling," 50 a. Wit: George Robeshaw, John Briggs. Acknowledged Sep 7 1675. Edward Sauvage, Clk. Power of Atty from Thomas Phillips to Robert Evans to acknowledge deed. Witnessed by William Winsmore and John Richardson. Acknowledged by Thomas Phillips Sep 7 1675. Edward Sauvage, Clk. Power of Atty from William Simpson to Thomas Williams to receive acknowledgement. Witnessed by William Winsmore, John Richardson. Acknowledged Sep 7 1675. Edward Sauvage, Clk.

1 Old 176/Sep 13 1675/Henry Turner to John Jolley: Agreement to execute deed for 150 a. of land. Wit: A. Wright, John Wright.

1 Old 176/Oct 6 1670/Robert Harwood of Miles River, Talbot County, to William Worgin and Alice his wife of Fishing Creek in Little Choptank River: 150 a., moyety or 1/2 of a tract of land called "Harwood's Choice" on Fishing Creek and Little Choptank River, adj land of Stephen Gary. Wit: Anthony Dawson, Stephen Gary. Acknowledged Mar 7 1670. Edward Sauvage, Clk.

1 Old 178/Feb 15 1670/Raymond Staplefort to William Broughton: 100 a. called "Staplefort's Lott" on Hungar River patented to sd Staplefort. Wit: Thomas Taylor, A. Wright. Acknowledged by Raymond Staplefort and Elinor his wife Mar 7 1670. Edward Sauvage, Clk. Power of Atty from Elinor Staplefort to William Jones. Wit: Richard Millington, Samuel Millington, James Crosses, Nicholas Bonn, Edw. Hughes, Nicholas Smith, Henry Grunnadg.

1 Old 181/Mar 30 1670/Henry Tripp to John Brooke: 150 a. between Jordan's Point and Manning's Point. Wit: Edward Sauvage, Stephen Gary. Acknowledged Mar 7 1670. Edward Sauvage, Clk.

1 Old 182/Mar 6 1670/Timothy Goodridge to Edward Roe: 200 a. on Cabin Creek, part of "Goodridge's Choice" patented to said Goodridge. Wit: Wm Battle, John Wright. Acknowledged Mar 7 1670. Edward Sauvage, Clk.

1 Old 183/Mar 6 1670/Timothy Goodridge to Wm Troth: 100 a. on Cabin Creek, part of "Goodridge's Choice" patented to said Goodridge; adj land formerly

sold by Goodridge to Wm Butler. Wit: John Wright, Wm Battle. Acknowledged
Mar 7 1670. Edward Sauvage, Clk.

1 Old 184/Mar 6 1670/Timothy Goodridge to Wm Butler: 100 a. on Cabin Creek,
part of "Goodridge's Choice." Wit: Daniell Clark, William Willoby. Acknowledged Mar 7 1670. Edward Sauvage, Clk.

1 Old 185/Jun 1 1670/Robert Gold and Nicholas Hackett to James Jones: Land on
Nanticoke River, 300 a. more or less. Wit: Wm Fowler, John Edmondson, Edw.
Roe. Acknowledged Aug 1 1670. Edward Sauvage, Clk. Daniell Clark, Atty for
Grantors; John Edmondson, Atty for Grantee.

1 Old 186/Nov 29 1671/Robert Seale to Arthur Wright: Power of Atty re 50 a.
called "Musketta Quarter." Wit: Francis Twyford, Margaret Chattle. Nov 7th,
- Peter Sharpe and Judith his wife of Calvert County, Chirurgeon, acknowledged Arthur Wright his Atty for lands sold by Sharpe to John Pollard.

1 Old 187/Feb 1 1668/John Attkins to Thomas Taylor of Patuxent River: Bond
for "50 acres of land and one shallop of twenty foot by ye keell." Wit: Hugh
Sherwood, John Hunt.

1 Old 187/Apr 16 1676/William Jones to Richard Kendall and John Early:
"Sealva's Chance" on Hungar River, containing 50 a. more or less. Jone, wife
of William Jones. Wit: William Barrington, John Offley.
Apr 11 167- John Kimball and Jone (Joane) his wife, formerly wife of Wm
Jones, deceased, to Richard Kendall and John Early: Dower Interest in
"Sealva's Chance." Wit: Raymond Stapleford of ye Quo., John Offley, Com.
Bond and receipt dated Apr 16-17, 1678. Witnessed by Richard Tubman, John
Offley.

1 Old 190/Jan 2 1682/Thomas Smithson to John LeCompte: "Royall," adj land of
John Edmondson called "Discovery." 50 a. more or less. Acknowledged Feb 7
1682/3 before Henry Trippe, Wm Stephens.

1 Old 191/Mar 5 1682/Bartholomew Ennalls to John Hayward: Part of 500 a. of
land bought of John Edmondson called "Beaver Neck," adj land of Wm Merchant
called "Merchant's Adventure," containing 200 a. more or less. Wit: Obadiah
King, Edw. Willson. Acknowledged Mar 7 1682. Thomas Smithson, Clk.

1 Old 192/Mar 7 1682/John Taylor to James Pattison: Part of "Armstrong's
Quarter," containing by patent 200 a., on Oyster Creek. 100 a. conveyed.
Wit: Henry Howard, John Hungerford. Priscilla, wife of John Taylor. Acknow-
ledged Mar 7 1682. Thomas Smithson, Clk.

1 Old 193/Mar 7 1682/James Pattison to John Taylor: Part of "Dover" contain-
ing by patent 150 a. on Oyster Creek in Taylor's Island adj "Armstrong's
Quarter." 47 a. conveyed. Wit: John Hungerford, Henry Howard. Acknowledged
Mar 7 1682. Thomas Smithson, Clk.

1 Old 195/Feb 8 1682/James Noell and Margaret Noell his wife to John Pope:
"Oyster Point" adj Anthony Lecompte's land and "Castle Haven." Acknowledged
Feb 8 1682. Thomas Smithson, Clk.

1 Old 196/Aug 4 1683/John Booth to Thomas Smithson of Talbot County, Gent.:
"Arcadia" at the head of a branch of Chicamocomico. Wit: Henry Howard,
Anthony Thompson. Acknowledged Aug 9 1683. Thomas Smithson, Clk.

2 Old 1/Aug 11 1719/William Cawsey to James Hayes: Part of "Tench's Range,"
40 a. on Chicamocomico. Wit: John Weber, Edward Trippe. Acknowledged Aug
11 1719 before Capt. John Rider and his assoc. Justices. Goovt. Loockerman,
Clk.

2 Old 2/Aug 12 1719/Arthur Whitly and Jone (Joan) his wife to Thomas Nevett,
Merchant: 2 a. of land in the Town of Cambridge; also a tract of 16 a. of
land oalled "St. Anthony" near Cambridge adj "White Lodge," "Cambridge
Addition" and "Rickerton." Wit: Goovert Loockerman, John Robson. Acknow-
ledged Aug 12 1719 before John Rider and Charles Nutter, Justices. Goovt.
Loockerman, Clk.

2 Old 3/Aug 12 1719/Thomas Hunt, Mariner, and Ann his wife to Walter Campbell,
Gent.: "Timber Point," 100 a. more or less on Fishing Creek & Little Choptank
River, adj "Gary's Choice." Wit: Thomas Hayward, Thomas Peirson. Acknow-
ledged Aug 12 1719 by Thomas Hunt before Col. Roger Woolford and assoc.
Justices. Goovt. Loockerman, Clk. Acknowledged Aug 12 1719 by Anne Hunt
before Henry Tripp and John Meekins.

2 Old 4/Isaac and John Nicolls, Planters, to their brother Joseph Nicolls:
100 a., part of "Richerson's Choice" on Marshy Creek adj land granted to
Benjamin Nicolls & adj land of Rice Levinus. Acknowledged Aug 13 1719 before
Capt. John Rider and assoc. Justices. Goovt. Loockerman, Clk.

2 Old 4/July 20 1719/Joseph Nicolls, Planter, and Margaret his wife to
Joseph Alford: 100 a., part of "Richardson Choice" adj land of Benjamin
Nicolls. Wit: Isaac Nicolls, Richard Webster. Acknowledged Aug 13 1719
before Capt. John Rider and assoc. Justices. Goovert Loockerman, Clk.

2 Old 5/Nov 11 1719/Thomas Lynes, Planter, and Elizabeth his wife to William
Houlton, Taylor: "Moadsleys Addition," 100 a. on the road from Staplefort's
Creek to Dr. Kingsbury's plantation. Wit: Richard Webster, Abraham Gambrall.
Acknowledged Nov 11 1719 before Major Henry Ennalls and assoc. Justices.
Goovert Loockerman, Clk.

2 Old 7/Mar 26 1719/Charles Bradley Sr and his son Charles Bradley Jr to
Henry Davis, Planter: Part of "Edmondson's Reserve" formerly belonging to
Richard Thompson, containing 100 a. Wit: William Ellis, Joseph Blackwell,
Richard Foster. Acknowledged Nov 11 1719 before Major Henry Ennalls and
assoc. Justices. Goovert Loockerman, Clk.

2 Old 8/Nov 11 1719/Arthur Whitly to Michael Deen: 100 a. called "Turner's
Adventure" on a branch of Hunting Creek. Wit: John Gray, William Hatfield Sr.
Acknowledged Nov 11 1719 before Major Henry Ennalls and associate Justices.
Goovert Loockerman, Clk.

2 Old 9/Nov 12 1719/John Robson to his son in law and daughter, Richard and
Mary Chapman: "Armstrong's Quarter" containing 200 a. on Taylor's Island on
the cove of Oyster Creek. Wit: Richard Webster, W. Clarkson. Acknowledged
Nov 12 1719 before Major Henry Ennalls and assoc. Justices. Goovert Loockerman, Clk.

2 Old 9/Nov 12 1719/Thomas Brown and Naomi Brown his wife, Carpenter, to
Samuel Dickinson, Merchant: 1/2 of 300 a. called the "Plains" on Hunting
Creek. Wit: Walter Quinton, Thomas Hews. Acknowledged by Thomas Browne and
John Kirke, Atty for Naomi Brown, before Major Henry Ennalls and assoc.
Justices. Goovert Loockerman, Clk.

2 Old 11/Nov 12 1719/Isaac Nichols to William Chipley: Part of "Richerson's Choyce" adj land of Rice Levenus; containing 120 a. more or less. Wit: John Lane, Abraham Gamble. Acknowledged Nov 12 1719 before Roger Woolford and assoc. Justices. Goovert Loockerman, Clk.

2 Old 12/Sep 20 1719/George Kirkman, Planter, and Eliza his wife to Richard Hart, Planter: "George's Delight" on Cedar Creek and Fishing Bay, containing 50 a. more or less. Wit: Richard Webster, William Webster. Acknowledged Nov 12 1719 before Major Henry Ennalls and assoc. Justices. Goovert Loockerman, Clk.

2 Old 13/Nov 13 1719/Charles Thompson, Planter to Anthony Rawlings, Planter: "Thompson's Lott, on Transquaking River between "Friendship" and "Rawlings Range" containing 19 a. more or less. Wit: John Cooke, William Houlton. Acknowledged Nov 13 1719 before Major Henry Ennalls and assoc. Justices. Goovert Loockerman, Clk.

2 Old 13/Nov 10 1719/Mary Rawley, Widow to William Ennalls: Part of "Taylor's Chance" on Cicamocomico, containing 260 a. more or less. Wit: John Dawson, Thomas ___. Acknowledged Nov 12 1719 before Levin Hicks and John Keene, Justices.

2 Old 14/Oct 9 1718/Josias Bradley and Margaret his wife to William Ennalls: Lot in Vienna, lot 47 on plat of town, containing 3/4 a. Wit: Thomas Colson, William Rolley. Acknowledged Dec 22 1719 by James Hayes, atty for grantors, before Walter Campbell and Capt. Henry Trippe, Justices.

2 Old 15/Jan 29 1719/John Ross and Frances his wife to Thomas Smith: "John's Lott" on N.W. side of Northwest Fork of Nanticoke, containing 50 a. more or less. Wit: Henry Ennalls, Charles Nutter. Acknowledged Jan 29 1719 before Henry Ennalls and Charles Nutter, Justices.

2 Old 16/Feb 2 1718/Thomas Gray and Mary his wife to William Jones: "Goodridge's Choice" on Cabin Creek, containing 101 a. more or less. Wit: Richard Hooper, Bartholomew Ennalls, Henry Ennalls. Acknowledged Feb 2 1718 before Henry Ennalls and Levin Hicks, Justices, by Thomas Gray. Acknowledged Jun 10 1719 by Mary, wife of Thomas Gray, before Roger Woolford and assoc. Justices. Goovert Loockerman, Clk.

2 Old 18/Sep 21 1719/Letter of Atty from Thomas Tyrer and Owen Pritchard of Liverpool, merchants, to Thomas Nevett of Little Choptank, merchant. Wit: James McMullen, Thos Harrison. Ralph Peters, Notary. Proved Feb 2 1719 by James McMullen before Walter Campbell and Henry Ennalls.

2 Old 18/Mar 8 1719/Levin Hicks, Gent. to Hugh Handley, Planter: "Levin's Chance" on Chicamocomico adj a tract called "Sector" and containing 25 a. more or less. Wit: Thomas Reed, Richd Webster, John Davis. Acknowledged Mar 8 1719 before Walter Campbell and assoc. Justices. Goovert Loockerman, Clk.

2 Old 19/Mar 12 1719/John King, Carpenter, to Henry Ennalls, Gent.: "Friendship" on Transquaking River, containing 135 a. more or less. Wit: John Kirke, John Edmondson, Thomas Hayward. Acknowledged Mar 12, 1719 before Walter Campbell and assoc. Justices. Goovert Loockerman, Clk.

2 Old 21/Dec 28 1719/Thomas Howell, Gent. to John Orrell, Merchant: Lot in Cambridge, the fourth lot by the record & plat of the said Town, containing about 3/4 a. Mary, wife of Thomas Howell. Wit: Charles Unger, John Davis. Acknowledged Mar 12 1719 before Walter Campbell and assoc. Justices. Goovert Loockerman, Clk.

2 Old 22/Feb 29 1719/John Nutter of Sussex County, Pennsylvania, and Mary his wife to Charles Nutter of Dorchester, Gent.: 400 a., part of a tract of 1200 a. called "Attowattocoqum" on Nanticoke, devised by Christopher Nutter of Somerset County, grandfather of Grantor, to be equally divided between John Nutter, Father, and Charles and William Nutter, Uncles of Grantor. (Christopher and Matthew Nutter of Somerset County, Uncles of Grantor, Executors of Will of Christopher Nutter) Wit: John Bound, Jonathan Clifton. Acknowledged Mar 11 1719 before Walter Campbell and assoc. Justices by Goovert Loockerman, atty for grantors. Goovert Loockerman, Clk.

2 Old 23/Mar 9 1719/Thomas Taylor, Gent. to John Orrell, Merchant: Sixth Lot on plat of the Town of Cambridge. Wit: John Eccleston, Thos Eccleston. Acknowledged Mar 9 1719 before Henry Ennalls and Henry Trippe, Justices.

2 Old 25/Mar 9 1719/Thomas Hunt, Gent., and Anne his wife to John Standford: "Benjamin's Mess" on Blackwater River containing 23 a. more or less, adj "London" and "Hocady." Wit: Thomas Reed, John Young. Acknowledged Mar 12 1719 before Walter Campbell and Henry Ennalls, Justices.

2 Old 26/Mar 9 1719/John Keene Sr and Mary his wife to "My well beloved son Benjamin Keene": "Clark's Outhold" containing 100 a., being grantor's dwelling plantation on Salt Marsh Creek (Keene's Creek) wich issues out of
Slaughter Creek. Life estate reserved to grantors. Wit: Henry Ennalls, John Lawson, Charles Nutter. Acknowledged Mar 9 1719 before Henry Ennalls and Charles Nutter, Justices.

2 Old 26/Jun 14 1720/Philemon Phillips, planter and Allis his wife to Henry Orrell (Orreall): "Mount Silley" containing 108 a. more or less, "to be holden of ye Manner of Nanticoke" by Certificate of Survey dated Mar 11 1694. Wit: Walter Campbell, Thomas Taylor. Acknowledged Jun 14 1720 before Jacob Loockerman and associate Justices. Goovert Loockerman, Clk.

2 Old 27/Nov 15 1719/Jacob Gray, planter and Isabell his wife to William Jones: Part of "Guttridg Choice" on Cabin Creek containing 150 a. of land. Wit: Edward Verin, Goovert Loockerman. Assignment from Philadelphia Williams to William Jones of her "third part of ye within mentioned lands," dated Jun 15 1720. Acknowledged Jun 15 1720 before Jacob Loockerman and associate Justices. Goovert Loockerman, Clk.

2 Old 28/Mar 25 1717/Samuell Rawley, planter and Mary his wife to William Ennalls, Merchant: 1/2 of "Taylor's Chance" on Chicamocomico River containing 260 a. more or less. Wit: Thomas Taskett, William Rawley. Acknowledged Mar 25 1718 before John Rider and Levin Hicks, Justices.

2 Old 29/Jun 15 1720/Edward Alford, planter and Mary his wife to Samuell Dickenson: Part of "Fox Hill" and "Fox Hill Addition" on Marshy Creek, adj "Eldridge" and Richardson's Folly," containing 110 a. more or less. Wit: William Price, Arthur Whiteley, Michall Deane. Acknowledged Jun 15 1720 before Jacob Loockerman and assoc. Justices. Goovert Loockerman, Clk.

2 Old 30/Apr 16 1719/James Ponder and Rachell his wife to Charles Standford: Part of "Alexander's Place" on Transquaking River, containing 30 a. more or less . Wit: Henry Ennalls, Philip Feddeman. Acknowledged Jun 14 1720 by John Standford, atty for grantors, before Jacob Loockerman and assoc. Justices. Goovert Loockerman, Clk.

2 Old 32/Oct 27 1719/James Ponder and Rachell his wife to Charles Standford: Part of "Alexander's Place" containing 5 a. more or less. Wit: Henry Ennalls, Philip Feddeman. Acknowledged Jun 14 1720 by John Standford, Atty

for grantors, before Jacob Loockerman and assoc. Justices. Goovert Loockerman, Clk.

2 Old 33/Jun 14 1720/John Tench and Elizabeth his wife to John Hudson Secundus: Part of two tracts called "John's Delight" and "Tench's Range" on Chicamocomico River, containing 391 a. more or less. Wit: Isaac Nicholls, Stephen
Owens. Acknowledged Jun 14 1720 before Jacob Loockerman and assoc. Justices.
Goovert Loockerman, Clk.

2 Old 34/Jun 15 1720/William Holton and Ann his wife to Henry Haines, planter:
Part of a tract of land called "Mosley's Addition" on road that goes by the
head of Stapleford's Creek to Dr. Kingsbury's Plantation, containing 100 a.
more or less. Wit: Tho. Taylor, James Hayes. Acknowledged Jun 15 before
Jacob Loockerman and assoc. Justices. Goovert Loockerman, Clk.

2 Old 35/Jun 14 1720/John Tench and Elizabeth his wife to George Kirkman:
"End of All Strife" on SW side of NW Fork of Nanticoke, containing 60 a. more
or less. Wit: William Ennalls, James Sear. Acknowledged Jun 14 1720 before
Jacob Loockerman and assoc. Justices. Goovert Loockerman, Clk.

2 Old 36/Jun 14 1720/Edward Wright to James Langerill: Part of "White Chapple"
on main branch of Chi,cacone Creek containing 24 a. more or less. Wit: James
Hayes, John Ross. Acknowledged Jun 14 1720 before Jacob Loockerman and
assoc. Justices. Goovert Loockerman, Clk.

2 Old 37/Jun 14 1720/William Herrin Jr to Thomas Made: "Hermitage" containing
100 a. more or less on Water Creek on S. side of Choptank River. Originally
granted to Charles Brown. Wit: William Ellis, Stephen Owens. Acknowledged
Jun 15 1720 before Jacob Loockerman and assoc. Justices. Goovert Loockerman,
Clk.

2 Old 38/Jun 15 1720/William Ennalls and Anne his wife to Rebecca Peirson:
Part of "Ennalls Reserve" containing 45 a. on N. side of Transquaking River.
Wit: Richard Watts, Thomas Canner. Acknowledged Jun 15 1720 before Jacob
Loockerman and assoc. Justices. Goovert Loockerman, Clk.

2 Old 39/Jun 15 1720/Rebecca Peirson to John Eccleston: In consideration of
45 a. adj land where said Rebecca Peirson lives, she conveys a tract called
"Alexander's Place" containing 30 a. more or less. Wit: Richard Watts, Thos
Canner. Acknowledged Jun 15 1720 before Jacob Loockerman and assoc. Justices.
Goovert Loockerman, Clk.

2 Old 40/Feb 10 1719/Jacob Loockerman and Dorothy his wife to Patrick
Broughan: "Pig Point" on a branch of Blackwater River containing 50 a. more
or less. Wit: Thomas Hayward, John Lawson. Acknowledged Jun 16 1720 before
Walter Campbell and John Keene, Justices.

2 Old 41/Jun 15 1720/James Hayes to Morris Dugane: Part of "Hogg Range" adj
land of Thomas White and containing 50 a. more or less. Wit: James Jerrard,
Edward Trippe. Acknowledged Jun 15 1720 before Jacob Loockerman and assoc.
Justices. Goovert Loockerman, Clk.

2 Old 42/Jun 15 1720/Thomas Burke to Thomas Made: "Hermitage" containing 100
a. more or less, originally granted to Charles Brown. Wit: William Ellis,
Stephen Owens. Acknowledged Jun 15 1720 before Jacob Loockerman and assoc.
Justices. Goovert Loockerman, Clk.

2 Old 42/Mar 10 1719/Samuel Chew to John Orrell: Power of Atty. Wit: John
Harwood, Bazell Noell.

2 Old 43/Jun 17 1720/Thomas Howell to his son Thomas Howell: Negro man named
Will. Wit: John Keene, Phil. Feddeman. Acknowledged Jun 17 1720 before

Jacob Loockerman and assoc. Justices. Goovert Loockerman, Clk.

2 Old 43/Richard Tubman to his son Richard Tubman Jr: Four Negroes. Wit:
Edward Keene, Ezekiel Keene. Acknowldeged before Jacob Loockerman and John
Keene Sr.

2 Old 44/Jun 1 1720/John Richardson and Eliza his wife to William Thomas:
Part of "Goodridge Choice" on Cabin Creek containing 50 a. Wit: Goovert
Loockerman, Thomas Feddeman. Acknowledged Jun 1 1720 before Henry Ennalls
and Henry Trippe, Justices.

2 Old 45/Jul 25 1720/William Nutter of Dorchester County and Robert Jones of
Somerset County, Atty in Fact of John Nutter of Pennsylvania, to John Rider
of Dorchester County: Inconsideration of a tract of 361 a. called "Doublin"
and Twenty Pounds in cash, they convey "Hansel" on Taylors Creek and Nanticoke River containing 700 a. more or less. Wit: William Ennalls, Philip
Feddeman, Thos Hicks Jr. Alce, wife of William Nutter. Acknowledged Jul
25 1720 before Henry Ennalls and Levin Hicks, Justices. Power of Atty from
John Nutter to Robert Jones, dated Jul 14 1720. Witnessed by John Crockett
and John Hines. Proved Jul 25 1720 before Henry Ennalls and Levin Hicks,
Justices.

2 Old 47/Aug 10 1720/John Hodson Secundus to Edward Trippe: Part of "Tenches
Range" and "John's Delight" conveyed to Hodson by deed dated Jun 14 1720,
adj land of James Hayes and containing 177 a. more or less. Wit: John Hodson
Jun., James Hayes. Acknowledged Aug 10 1720 before Jacob Loockerman and
assoc. Justices. Goovert Loockerman, Clk.

2 Old 47/Aug 9 1720/John Hodson Secundus to James Hayes: Part of "Tenches
Range" and "John's Delight" conveyed to Hodson by deed dated Jun 14 1720,
containing 214 a. more or less. Wit: Jno Griffin, Jno Cole. Acknowledged
Aug 10 1720 before Jacob Loockerman and assoc. Justices. Goovert Loockerman,
Clk.

2 Old 48/Aug 6 1720/John Hodson Senior to his brother John Hodson Secundus:
Grave Yard containing 6 a., part of a tract on the North side of Chicamoco-
mico called "Second Addition Corrected." Wit: Hugh Handly, Joseph Haines.
Acknowledged Aug 12 1720 before Jacob Loockerman and assoc. Justices. Goovert
Loockerman, Clk.

2 Old 49/Aug 11 1720/Henry Davis and Elizabeth his wife to John Hubbart:
"Batchelors Loss," containing 47 a. more or less. Wit: Arthur Whiteley,
Thomas Tregoe. Acknowledged Aug 11 1720 before Jacob Loockerman and assoc.
Justices. Goovert Loockerman, Clk.

2 Old 50/Aug 11 1720/Johannas Dehinoyossa to Goovert Loockerman: "Rogues
Beguiled" containing 100 a. more or less. Wit: John Pitt, John Orrell.
Acknowledged Aug 12 1720 before Jacob Loockerman and assoc. Justices. Thos
Hayward, Clk.

2 Old 51/Aug 10 1720/Peter Taylor and Mary his wife to William Newell: "Bear
Garden" containing 35 a. more or less. Wit: Jacob Loockerman. Acknowledged
Aug 10 1720 before Jacob Loockerman and assoc. Justices. Goovert Loockerman,
Clk.

2 Old 52/Jul 25 1720/John Rider to William Nutter: Inconsideration of a tract
of 700 a. called "Hansel" lying in Chicacone Indian Town conveyed to John
Rider by William Nutter, "Doublin," containing 361 a. more or less, is
conveyed to Nutter. Wit: W. Ennalls, Phil. Feddeman, Charles Nutter. Acknowledged Jul 25 1720 by John Rider and Ann his wife before Henry Ennalls and
Levin Hicks, Justices.

2 Old 53/Jul 1 1720/Nicholas Sewell of St. Mary's County, Gent., to Henry
Hooper of Dorchester County, Mariner: "Warwick" on Secretary Creek containing
1000 a. more or less. Also "Secretary's Point" containing 200 a. on Cabin
Creek and Secretary Creek, and all of Sewell's interest in any land lying
between Secretary Creek and Cabin Creek alias Sewell's Creek. Henry Sewell
and Jane Sewell alias Calvert, father and mother of Nicholas Sewell. Wit:
Nicholas Sewell Junr., Thomas Hooper, James Hailes. William Murray, Atty
for Nicholas Sewell. Acknowledged Aug 10 1720 before Jacob Loockerman and
assoc. Justices. Goovert Loockerman, Clk.

2 Old 55/July 25 1720/Robert Jones of Somerset County, Atty in fact of John
Nutter of Sussex County, Pennsylvania, to Charles Nutter of Dorchester County:
"Tossewandake" containing 130 a. near head of Nanticoke; and 400 a., being
1/3 of a tract of 1200 a. called "Attowattocoquin" at the head of Nanticoke.
Wit: William Ennalls, Philip Feddeman, Thomas Hicks Junr. Acknowledged Jul
25 1720 before Henry Ennalls and Levin Hicks, Justices.

2 Old 56/Jul 25 1720/Robert Jones, Atty in fact for John Nutter, to William
Nutter of Dorchester County: 1/3 of "Attowattocoquin" containing 1200 a. in
all, 400 a. being conveyed. Wit: William Ennalls, Philip Feddeman, Thomas
Hicks Junr., William Murray. Acknowledged Jul 25 1720 before Henry Ennalls
and Levin Hicks, Justices.

2 Old 57/Jul 25 1720/Christopher Nutter of Somerset County, Gent. and Robert
Jones, Atty for John Nutter, to Christopher Nutter, brother of said John
Nutter and Sarah his wife: 239 a. called "Rich Ridge" near the head of Nanti-
coke River, granted to Christopher Nutter, having descended at his death to
"the said Christopher Nutter his second son and the said John Nutter his
Grandson by his first son John Nutter then deceased." Conveyed to Christo-
pher Nutter and Sarah his wife for their lifetime and then to their sons,
Christopher and Matthew. Wit: Phil Feddeman, W. Ennalls, Thomas Hicks Junr.
Acknowledged Jul 25 1720 before Henry Ennalls and Levin Hicks, Justices.

2 Old 59/Aug 24 1719/Thomas Hicks Sr and Sarah his wife to Elias Venalson:
"Hicks Lott" patented to said Thomas Hicks Jun 5 1687 on the North side of
Nanticoke at the mouth thereof, containing 17 a. and 112 square perches, more
or less. Wit: John Read, John Rider, Levin Hicks. Acknowledged Aug 24 1719
before John Rider and Levin Hicks, Justices.

2 Old 60/Aug 24 1717/William Green of Dorchester County, planter, to John
Reed of Somerset County, planter: "Poate" containing 50 a. granted to Green
on Apr 5 1684 on West side of Nanticoke. Wit: John Rider, Levin Hicks.
Acknowledged Aug 24 1719 before John Rider and Levin Hicks, Justices.

2 Old 61/Sep 1 1720/John Bullen of Dorchester County, planter, to Richard
Peerson Junr. of said County, planter: "Turkey Point" in Black Water containing 350 a. more or less. Wit: Thomas Brannock, William Philips. Acknowledged Nov 11 1720 before Jacob Loockerman and assoc. Justices. Goovert
Loockerman, Clk.

2 Old 62/Nov 8 1720/Richard Webster to Edward Varing: Part of "Busby" con-
taining by estimation 70 a. of land. Signed by Richard Webster and Anne
Webster. Wit: Shad. Feddeman, William Jones. Acknowledged Nov 10 1720 by
Richard Webster before Jacob Loockerman and assoc. Justices. Goovert
Loockerman, Clk.

2 Old 63/1720/William Green, Sr, to John Rider: "Marsh Island" on North side
of Nanticoke containing 173 a.; "Green Privilege" on North side of Nanticoke
between Oyster Creek and Fishing Creek containing 70 a. and 3 Roods; and

"Green's Adventure" on North side of Nanticoke containing 100 a. more or less.
Wit: William Burn, William Hously. Acknowledged Dec 22 1720 before Major
Henry Ennalls and Mr. Peter Taylor, Justices, by Thomas Hicks Sr, atty in
fact for William Green Sr.

2 Old 66/Nov 1 1720/John Cotterell of Northumberland County, Virginia,
Planter, and Lucretia his wife, to Ambrose Aaron of Dorchester County,
Planter: "The Commencement" on an island in Slaughter Creek adj land of
Raymond Staplefort and St. John's Creek, containing 100 a. more or less.
Wit: William Robson, John Meekins. Acknowledged Nov 16 1720 be Robert Reid,
Atty for grantors, beofre Roger Woolford and John Robson, Justices.

2 Old 67/Nov 1 1720/John Cotterell and Lucretia his wife to John Meekins:
"Taylor's Inheritance" on Taylors Island in Slaughter Creek and St. John's
Creek, containing 200 a. more or less. Wit: William Robson, Ambrose Aaron.
Acknowledged Nov 16 1720 by Robert Reid, Atty for grantors, before Roger
Woolford and John Robson, Justices.

2 Old 69/Aug 16 1720/John Kirk and Anthony Rawlings to John Orrell: Third
Lot in Cambridge, containing about 3/4 a. Wit: James Hayes, P. Feddeman.
Acknowledged Oct 22 1720 by John Kirk before Henry Ennalls and Henry Trippe,
Justices. Acknowledged Nov 8 1720 by Anthony Rawlings before John Keene and
Charles Nutter, Justices.

2 Old 70/"Dorchester County, Sct.
   "The Deposition of Mr. James Peterkin aged about seventy seven years or
thereabouts Being swore on the Holy Evangelist Saith that he did att the
request of a certain Joseph Sargent publickly read his Last Will and Testament to him several Times in the presence and hearing of severall of his
neighbours Particularly John Draper and John Young they were desired to sine
as Evidences to the said will with my self the which will bearing date the
12th day of July One thousand six hundred Eighty five which he the said
Joseph Sargent Declared to be his Last Will and Testament and att that Time
this Deponent further saith that the said Joseph Sargent att the time when
they were goeing to sine the Will as Evidences that he Desired them to for-
bear a Little & called his Daughter Rebecca to him and laid his hand on her
head and Desired them to take notice that was his child that he had given ｨand
bequeath all his land to Let her be called by what name so ever and this ｣
deponent further saith not.
June 14th 1714 Sworn and Examined Before me the Subscriber one of her
Majestie's Justices for the said County. Henry Ennalls"

2 Old 70/1720/Proceedings re real estate of Thomas Tyrer, deceased, Bankrupt:
On complaint of Samuel Powell of Liverpool for himself and other creditors of
Thomas Tyrer, a Commission is issued to John Ratcliffe and Thomas Willis,
Esqs. and Ralph Peters, Henry Orme and James Gordon, Gent., Commissioners of
Bankrupt. Assignment from Thomas Willis, Ralph Peters and Henry Orme, Com-
missioners, to Samuel Powell and William Cleiveland, Trustees: All the real
and personal estate of Thomas Tyrer, deceased, in trust for the benefit of
the creditors of said Tyrer. Power of Atty from William Cleiveland and
Samuel Powell to John Sinnott and William Williamson as to property of Tyrer
in Virginia and Maryland. Witnessed by Thomas Jones, Thomas Brillon, William
Taylor. Ralph Peters, Notary Public. Henry Taylor, Esq., "Majr. of ye
Burrough and Corporation of Liverpool." Proved by oath of Thomas Jones
before Henry Ennalls and John Robson, Justices, May 16 1721.

2 Old 76/Nov 22 1720/John Leverton of Talbot County, Cooper to Matthew Parramore of Dorchester County: "Leverton's Choice" containing 202 a. more or less, adj land formerly surveyed for Col. Lee. Wit: Thoas Fisher, W. Turbutt. Acknowledged Nov 22 1720 before Thos Fisher and W. Turbutt, Justices for Queen Anne's County.

2 Old 77/Mar 17 1720/John Rider and Anne his wife to George Staplefort: "Bull Point" on the north side of Bohemia Back Creek which issues out of the SW side of NW Branch of Blackwater River, on both sides of said River, containing 71 a. more or less. Wit: G. Loockerman, John Davis. Acknowledged by John Rider Mar 18 1720 before Henry Ennalls and assoc. Justices. Goovert Loockerman, Clk.

2 Old 79/Apr 14 1720/Mary Barratt of the City of London, Widow, to Henry Trippe of Dorchester County: "Bath" on Secretary Creek, 1010 a. more or less; and "Addition to Bath" adj "Bath," containing 622 a. more or less. Except 299 a. of "Bath" (part of the above mentioned 1010 a.) formerly granted to Philip Taylor and sold by him to Francis Anderton. "Addition to Bath" contains 397 a. claimed by the Indians. Wit: Moses Rawlings, Henry Sampson, Stephen Yoakley. Acknowledged in open Court by William Smith of Calvert County for Mary Barratt, before Henry Ennalls and assoc. Justices. Goovert Loockerman, Clk.

2 Old 81/Mar 14 1720/Josias Mace and Angell his wife, William Wroten and Hannah his wife to Nicholas Mace, Sr: "Cedar Point" on S. side of Little Choptank River, on the East side of Fishing Creek, containing 200 a. Acknowledged Mar 15 1720 by Josias Mace for himself and as Atty for William Wroten and Hannah his wife, before Jacob Loockerman and assoc. Justices. Goovert Loockerman, Clk. Power Atty dated Feb 22 1720, witnessed by John Robson and Roger Woolford.

2 Old 82/Nov 15 1720/Garratt Garratson of Christeen (Christian) Creek in New Castle County, Delaware, and Esther his wife, daughter and surviving heir of Edward Bell late of Dorchester County, deceased, to Walter Quinton of Talbot County: "Heram" on S side of Great Choptank River and on the S side of Ingrams Creek, adj 300 a. laid out for Walter Dickenson and containing 45 a. more or less; also "Bunnell Fields" between Ingrams Creek and Watts Creek, 50 a. adj "Morefields Addition" laid out for William Troth. Wit: Amey Doughty, Henry Sapp. Acknowledged by JohnKirk, Atty for Garratt Garrattson, before Jacob Loockerman and assoc. Justices. Goovert Loockerman, Clk.

2 Old 85/1720/Thomas Vickers and Eliza his wife to Abraham Mitchell: "Paradice" on Little Choptank and Fishing Creek, near "Papaw Thcikett" and containing 50 a. more or less. Wit: Arthur Whitley, Elizabeth Mitchell. Acknowledged Mar 14 1720 before Jacob Loockerman and assoc. Justices. Goovert Loockerman, Clk.

2 Old 86/Mar 16 1720/John Kirk and Sarah his wife to Charles Ungle: 1-1/2 a. in Cambridge called "Markett Place," adj land where the Parish Church stands. Wit: G. Loockerman, Richard Webster. Acknowledged Mar 16 1720 before Jacob Loockerman and assoc. Justices. Goovert Loockerman, Clk.

2 Old 87/Feb 9 1720/Thomas Taylor to Katherine Vaughoone: "Batheldors Hope" near the head of Cabin Creek, containing 220 a. more or less. Wit: John White, John Eccleston. Acknowledged Feb 14 1720 before Henry Ennalls and Peter Taylor, Justices.

2 Old 88/Oct 1 1720/John Cattrell of Northumberland County, Virginia to
William Robson: "Commencement" on an island in St. John's Creek, containing
100 a. more or less. Wit: John Meekins, Ambrose Aaron. Acknowledged Nov
16 1720 by Robert Reade, Atty for John Cottrell and Lucretia his wife, before
Roger Woolford and John Robson, Justices.

2 Old 90/Jan 5 1720/Edward Alford, planter, to Daniel Croney, planter: "Skipton" at the head of Fox Creek, adj land of John Edmondson and containing 200
a. more or less. Wit: James Keddar, John Sharp. Acknowledged Jan 5 1720
before Henry Ennalls and Henry Trippe, Justices.

2 Old 91/Mar 15 1720/Anthony Rawlings and Katherine his wife, John Charlescraft and Rebecca his wife, Charles Stanford and Mary his wife, and John
Eccleston to Andrew Smith, Carpenter: 16 a., part of "Alexanders Place."
Wit: William Smith, William Wheyland, Thomas Ennalls. Acknowledged Mar 16
1720 before Majr. Henry Ennalls and assoc. Justices. Goovert Loockerman, Clk.

2 Old 93/Jan 31 1720/Thomas Curtis of Talbot County to Thomas Edmondson:
"Dorchester," containing 700 a. on the North side of Edmondson's Creek,
excepting 100 a. in the occupation of John Fleharty; also 100 a. on the North
side of Edmondson's Creek. Wit: James Loyd, James Earle. Acknowledged Jan
31 1720 before James Loyd and William Clayton, Justices of Talbot County.
Phil Feddeman, Clark of Talbot County.

2 Old 94/John Keene, Sr, and Mary his wife to Benjamin Keene, son of Grantor:
"Keene's Neck" containing 250 a. near the head of Hungar River. Wit: Thomas
Hooper, James Butte. Acknowledged Nov 17 1720 before Roger Woolford and John
Robson, Justices.

2 Old 95/1719/Robert Jones and Mary his wife to William Ennalls: Sixth Lot in
Vienna, containing 3/4 a. Wit: Thomas Taylor, Thomas Hayward, John Eccleston.
Acknowledged Feb 14 1720 before Henry Ennalls and Peter Taylor, Justices.

2 Old 95/Apr 12 1721/Eliza Wetherell, Widow, to her three chidren, Edward
Barricraft, Mary Barricraft and Grace Wetherell: Personalty. Edward Barricraft, deceased husband of said Eliza Wetherell.

2 Old 96/Oct 3 1721/John Harwood and Rebecca his wife to their son, Thomas
Brannock: "Canterbury" on Transquakin River, after the death of his mother,
Rebecca, now the wife of John Harwood. Acknowledged Oct 3 1721 before Jacob
Loockerman and Henry Ennalls, Justices.

2 Old 96/Jun 15 1720/Joshua Morgan and Elizabeth his wife to Zachariah
Goforth of Kent County on Delaware Bay: "Morgan's Venture" containing 120 a.
more or less. Wit: Thomas Taylor, John Cullen. Acknowledged May 29 1721
before John Rider and Charles Nutter, Justices.

2 Old 97/Nov 17 1721/Edward Billiter and Anne his wife, intheir own right
and as attorneys for John Sumerly, to William Trippe: "Guinney Plantation,"
100 a. more or less, adj "Gotham" and "Sark." Acknowledged Nov 14 1721
before Jacob Loockerman and assoc. Justices. Goovert Loockerman, Clk.
Power of Atty from John Sumerly, son of Thomas Sumerly of London, deceased,
and of Mary his wife, also deceased, who was the daughter of Francis Soane
deceased and niece of his brother Joseph Soane deceased, to Edward Billiter
and Anne his wife, brother and sister of said John Sumerly. Witnessed by
William Greenwood, Joseph Riddall, Marm. Hendry. Proved before Robert Grundy
and W. Clayton, Justices for Talbot County, by William Greenwood and Joseph
Redwell. baptismal certificate of Mary, daughter of Francis Sone, baptized
Jan 3 1632. William Taswell, Rector of St. Mary Newington, Surrey. Wit:

Marm. Hendry, Atty and No. Publ. Marriage certificate of Thomas Somerly and Mary Sone, married Apr 22 1656 at the Parish Church of St. James's Dukes place. John Avery, Clk. Wit: Marm. Hendry, Atty and No. Publ. Burial certificate of Mary Sumerly, buried Jul 4 1698 at the Parish church of St. Paul Shadwell. John Hendry, Deputy Clarke. Wit: Marm. Hendry, Atty and No. Publ. Birth certificate of John, son of Thomas Sumerly and Mary his wife, born June 5 and baptized Jun 6 1666 at the parish church of St. Paul Shadwell. John Hendry, Deputy Clarke. Wit: Marm. Hendry, Atty and No. Publ.

2 Old 99/Jun 23 1721/Edmond Huggins of Somerset County and Anne his wife to Henry Smith of Dorchester County: "Poplar Neck" on N.W. side of Nanticoke River above Dadwins Creek and Martins Hundred, containing 75 a. more or less. Wit: James Cannon, Thomas Cannon. Acknowledged Jun 23 1721 before John Rider and Charles Nutter, Justices.

2 Old 100/Nov 1721/Thomas Pitt and Sarah his wife to Mark Fisher: "Barron Point" on Blackwater River, containing 40 a. more or less. Wit: Richard Webster, Joseph Alford. Acknowledged Nov 15 1721 before Jacob Loockerman and assoc. Justices. G. Loockerman, Clk.

2 Old 101/Nov 13 1721/William Kirke to David Peterkin: "Kirkes Wolfe Trapp" on N.W. fork of Nanticoke River. Acknowledged Nov 16 1721 before Jacob Loockerman and assoc. Justices. G. Loockerman, Clk.

2 Old 101/Aug 31 1720/Henry Owens and Ann his wife to Richard Price: "long Acre" in the fork of Nanticoke River, containing 100 a. more or less, adj land formerly belonging to Col. Lee of Virginia. Wit: Thomas Tackett, Henry Dyas. Acknowledged Nov 15 1721 by Samuel Cratcher, atty for Grantors, before Jacob Loockerman and assoc. Justices. G. Loockerman, Clk.

2 Old 102/Aug 15 1721/John Shapley of Virginia to Daniel Fallin of Dorchester County: "Westleigh Neck" on Fox Creek which issues out of Hungar River, containing 200 a. Wit: John Keene, Charles Robson. Acknowledged Nov 17 1721 before Jacob Loockerman and assoc. Justices, by Goovert Loockerman, atty for John Shapley. Goovert Loockerman, Clk. Power of Atty locates land in "Armitage Hundred."

2 Old 104/Henry Oneale of the Colony of Virginia to Thomas Tackett: Power of Atty to convey to William Ennalls of Dorchester County 100 a. called "Mount Cilly" on the W. side of Blackwater River near the head of a branch of the said river. Wit: Bartho. Ennalls, John Eccleston. Proved in open Court Nov 16 1721. G. Loockerman, Clk.

2 Old 104/Jul 14 1720/Elizabeth Minner, Relict of Peter Minner deceased, to her three sons Peter, John and Richard Minner: Personal property. Wit: Anne Ennalls, W. Taylor.

2 Old 104/Mar 15 1721/Arthur Whiteley and Joane his wife to Roger Woollford: 100 a. called "Whittlewood" on Cabin Creek. Wit: John Orrell, Thomas Reed. Acknowledged Mar 15 1721 before Jacob Loockerman and assoc. Justices. G. Loockerman, Clk.

2 Old 105/Mar 14 1721/John Charlescraft and Rebecca his wife, relict of John Pierson, to William Ennalls: "Ennalls Reserve" on N.W. side of Transquakin River, containing 45 a. more or less, formerly conveyed by the said Ennalls to the said Rebecca Charlescraft as Rebecca Pierson. Wit: John Pitt, Thos Pierson. Acknowledged Mar 14 1721 before Jacob Loockerman and assoc. Justices. G. Loockerman, Clk.

2 Old 106/Mar 14 1721/Henry Turner of Dorchester County to Edward Billiter:
"Fancy" on the east side of Great Choptank River in the freshes, and on the
east side of the S.E. branch of Phillips Creek, adj "Doncaster" and "Edmond-
son's Reserve" and containing 100 a. Wit: Joseph Alford, Richard Addams.
Acknowledged Mar 14 1721 by Henry Turner and Elizabeth his wife before Jacob
Loockerman and assoc. Justices. G. Loockerman, Clk.

2 Old 106/Mar 14 1721/John Charlescraft, planter, and Rebecca his wife to
John Pitt, Mariner: "Refuge" containing 50 a. on the N.W. side of Transquakin
River, adj "Strawberry Garden." Wit: Antho. Rawlings, Thos Pierson Sr.
Acknowledged Mar 14 1721 before Jacob Loockerman and assoc. Justices. G.
Loockerman, Clk.

2 Old 107/Jan 9 1721/Thomas Collson and Margaret his wife to William Layton
Jr: "Glad Tower" at head of Nanticoke River containing 100 a. more or less.
Wit: John Dyer, Mary Dyer. Acknowledged Feb 12 1721 before Charles Nutter
and Peter Taylor, Justices.

2 Old 109/May 16 1721/Joseph Alford and Hannah his wife to Samuel Irland:
"Richardson's Choice" containing 100 a. more or less adj Benjamin Nicholls'
land. Wit: William Parry, Cornelius Johnson. Acknowledged Mar 13 1721
before Jacob Loockerman and assoc. Justices. G. Loockerman, Clk.

2 Old 109/Mar 13 1720/John Eccleston to Charles Stanford: Part of "Alexander's
Place"on Transquakin River, conatining 8 a. more or less, for the term of 65
years. Wit: L. Flowers, Richard Webster. Acknowledged Mar 14 1721 before
Jacob Loockerman and assoc. Justices. G. Loockerman, Clk.

2 Old 110/Feb 27 1720/Benjamin Parratt and Katherine his wife of Kent County
upon Delaware River in the Territories of Pennsylvania to James Willson of
Talbot County: Part of "Brotherly Kindness" containing 250 a. on Great Choptank River opposite Kings Creek, which was not sold or disposed of by William
Parratt, grandfather of said Benjamin Parratt. Wit: Thomas Berry, William
Thistlewood, James Willson Jr. Acknowledged Mar 14 1721 by William Edmondson,
atty for grantors, before Jacob Loockerman and assoc. Justices. G. Loockerman, Clk.

2 Old 111/Feb 1 1720/Philip Feddeman to Charles Bradley: Lease of 50 a.
called "Feddeman's Fancy" to the said Charles for his lifetime and the lifetime of Easter his wife. Wit: James Dawson.

2 Old 112/May 12 1722/William Robson to John Robson Jr and Roger Robson: Two
tracts called "Robson's Range" and "Fadingworth," "Robson's Range" lying on
Taylor's Island in Slaughter Creek and containing 100 a. more or less, and
"Fadingworth" lying near Slaughter Creek in Taylor's Island adj "Robson's
Delight" and containing 100 a. more or less. Jane Robson, wife of William
Robson. Wit: John Keene, John Robson. Acknowledged before John Keene and
John Robson, Justices.

2 Old 113/Apr 13 1722/John Baker of St. Mary's County to Thomas Nevett of
Dorchester County: "Steele's," containing 510 a. more or less, and "Foulkes
Delight" containing 250 a. at head of Hunting Creek. Wit: T. Davis, John
Orrell, Arthur Whiteley. Acknowledged Apr 13 1722 before John Mackall.

2 Old 113/May 15 1722/Isaac Nicholls, Planter, to Henry Hooper, Mariner:
"Anderton's Point" on Secretary's Creek containing 108 a. more or less. Also
"Nicolls Regulations" between Secretary Creek and Cabin Creek, containing 202
a. more or less. Wit: Henry Ennalls, John Robson. Acknowledged May 15 1722
before Henry Ennalls and John Robson.

2 Old 114/Jan 9 1721/Thomas Hollins (Hollings, Holland) and Mary his wife to William Woods, Planter: "Hope," laid out for William Spencer, containing 50 a. more or less. Wit: Henry Turner, Elizabeth Turner. Acknowledged Jun 13 1722 by William Bexley, Atty for Grantors, before John Rider and Peter Taylor, Justices. Power of Atty witnessed by Mary Sulivane and William Spencer and proved by oath of William Spencer before Charles Nutter and Peter Taylor, Justices.

2 Old 115/Jun 13 1722/Betty Caco, Queen of Ababco Indians and daughter of Winacaco, and Pemetasusk, daughter of Patch Youske and Queen of the Hatch Swampe Indians, with other Indians, to Goovert Loockerman: "Foulkes Content" adj the freehold of William Dorrington deceased called "Busby," also adj "Ricarton" and containing 228 a. more or less. Wit: Charles Nutter, Peter Taylor, Richard Willis. Acknowledged Jun 13 1722 before Charles Nutter and Peter Taylor, Justices.

2 Old 116/Jun 13 1722/Betty Caco, daughter of Winecaco and Queen of the Abaco Indians, and Pemetasusk, daughter of Patch Youske and Queen of the Hatch Swampe Indians, with other Indians, to Isaac Nicolls: land on Secretary Creek and Goose Creek, near land of Richard Watts and containing 250 a. more or less. Wit: Henry Trippe, G. Loockerman, Richard Willis. Acknowledged Jun 13 1722 before Charles Nutter and Peter Taylor, Justices.

2 Old 118/Jun 14 1722/John Kirke and Sarah his wife to Thomas Nevett: Land in Cambridge, adj land formerly sold by Kirke to Arthur Whiteley of which Nevett is now seized, also adj land sold by Hugh Eccleston to Charles Ungle, and land formerly sold by Kirke to Joseph Cottman and now vested in the heirs of Thomas Bruff. Wit: Francis Allen, G. Loockerman. Acknowledged Jun 14 1722 before Jacob Loockerman and assoc. Justices. G. Loockerman, Clk.

2 Old 119/Jun 13 1722/Anthony Rawlings, Sr, and Katherine his wife to William Ennalls: "Masons Hopyard" on W. side of Transquaking River, containing 100 a. more or less, being 2/3 of sd Hopyard. Wit: Anthony Rawlings Jr, Thomas Talbott, William Taylor. Acknowledged Jun 14 1722 before Jacob Loockerman and assoc. Justices, G. Loockerman, Clk.

2 Old 119/Jun 13 1722/Anthony Rawlings Jr to William Ennalls: Land on W. side of Transquaking River near head of Salsbury's Dam, between "Friendship" and "Rawlings Range," containing 20 a. more or less. Wit: Anthony Rawlings, Thomas Talbott, W. Taylor. Acknowledged Jun 13 1722 before Jacob Loockerman and assoc. Justices. G. Loockerman, Clk.

2 Old 120/Jun 13 1722/Thomas Abbott to William Ennalls: Part of "Fisher's Choice" purchased by William Abbott, deceased, father of grantor, from Dorrington Fisher, on E. side of Blackwater River, containing 300 a. Wit: Anthony Rawlings, Anthony Rawlings Jr, W. Taylor. Acknowledged Jun 13 1722 before Henry Ennalls and John Rider, Justices.

2 Old 121/Jun 7 1722/Vachel Denton of Annapolis to Richard Cooper of Talbot County: "Denton Holme" in Talbot County adj land of Col. Vincent Lowe called "Towton Field" and containing 600 a. more or less. Henry Denton, father of Vachel Denton. Wit: Michael Fletcher, John Edmondson, Richard Bruff. Power of Atty from Vachel Denton to Charles Ungle, Goovert Loockerman and John Lawson, proved before William Clayton and Daniel Sherwood, Justices of Talbot County. Deed acknowledged Jun 13 1722 by Charles Ungle and John Lawson, before Roger Woollford, Justice.

2 Old 122/Jun 7 1922/Joseph Boss (Boyce) of Sussex County, Pennsylvania and Mary his wife to Jonathan Clifton of Dorchester County: "Boyce Venter" at head of Nanticoke containing 100 a. more or less. Wit: Charles Nutter, James Hayes. Acknowledged Jun 12 1722 by Goovert Loockerman, Atty for grantors, before Jacob Loockerman and assoc. Justices. G. Loockerman, Clk.

2 Old 123/Apr 7 1722/Thomas Hunt and Anne his wife and John Kirke to William Murray: "Congum" on Black water branches near land laid out for Thomas Manning and containing 100 a. Also "Merchants Range" containing 50 a. more or less. Wit: G. Loockerman, Levin Hicks. Acknowledged Apr 7 1722 before Henry Ennalls and John Rider, Justices.

2 Old 124/Jun 11 1722/John Richardson and Elizabeth his wife to Simon Thomas: Part of "Britt's Hope" formerly surveyed for 600 a. on Hunting Creek, 150 a. being conveyed. Wit: Hodson 2ds., Thomas Peirson. Acknowledged Jun 13 1722 before Jacob Loockerman and assoc. Justices. G. Loockerman, Clk.

2 Old 125/Jun 13 1722/Peter Taylor to Thomas Howell, Rector, and Vestry of Great Choptank Parish: 2 a., part of a tract called "Range," on which stands the Chapel of Ease. Wit: Charles Nutter, Thomas Hayward. Acknowledged Jun 14 1722 before Jacob Loockerman and assoc. Justices. G. Loockerman, Clk.

2 Old 126/Jun 15 1722/Edward Stephens to his cousin, John Cooke: Part of "Pressbury Composition." Wit: W. Ennalls, Edward Wright. Acknowledged Jun 15 1722 before Jacob Loockerman and assoc. Justices. G. Loockerman, Clk.

2 Old 127/Jun 7 1722/Joseph Boyce of Dorchester County and Mary his wife to John Rudolphus Bundelin: "Batchelors Folly" on Nanticoke containing 100 a.; and "Good Luck" containing 100 a. on Nanticoke. Wit: Charles Nutter, James Hayes. Acknowledged Jun 14 1722 by Goovert Loockerman, Atty for Grantors, before Jacob Loockerman and assoc. Justices. G. Loockerman, Clk.

2 Old 129/Jun 15 1722/William Cullen and Sarah his wife to John LeCompte: "White Fryers" adj "Steward's Place" on a creek called "Steward's Beginning," containing 77 a. more or less. Wit: Nehemiah Beckwith, P. Eilbeck. Acknowledged Jun 15 1722 before Jacob Loockerman and assoc. Justices. G. Loockerman, Clk.

2 Old 129/Nov 15 1718/Indenture of William Rowland, son of Peter Rowland deceased, with the consent of Eleanor Rowland (Redding), mother of said William Rowland, to John LeCompte, to serve as apprentice until he arrives at the age of 21 years, "being at this Instant going of Twelve years of age." Wit: Nehemiah Beckwith, John Warner, Thomas Taylor.

2 Old 130/Jun 13 1722/Edward Alford to William Edmondson and Daniel Croneen: "Ranges." Wit: Joseph Blackwell, William Bexsey. Acknowledged Jun 13 1722 before Jacob Loockerman and assoc. Justices. G. Loockerman, Clk.

2 Old 131/Jun 12 1722/Nicholas Mace and Ann his wife to James Fookes: "Cedar Point" on Fishing Creek on S. side of Little Choptank River, containing 200 a. more or less, reserving a 20-foot square of ground for a burying place. Wit: Roger Woolford, Joshua Kennarly. Acknowledged Jun 14 1722 before Roger Woolford, Justice.

2 Old 132/Aug 15 1722/David Jenkins to John Harwood: 1/2 of "Castle Haven" conveyed by Peter Underwood to John Whiteley by deed dated Nov 2 1675 for 100 a., and devised by Whiteley to said David Jenkins by his Last Will and Testament dated Oct 6 1701. Wit: Richard Webster, John Davis, P. Eilbeck. Acknowledged Jun 15 1722 before Jacob Loockerman and assoc. Justices. G. Loockerman, Clk.

2 Old 133/1722/John Brannock and Thomas Brannock to John White: Part of "Discovery" on Great Choptank River and Ingrams Creek, containing 1184 a. 280 a. conveyed adj land of Walter Dickinson. Wit: John Harwood, John Brannock Jr, Thomas Brannock Jr. Power of Atty from John Brannock and Margrett Brannock his wife to Thomas Brannock to convey 300 a., being part of a tract called "Discovery," to John White. Witnessed by John Abbott, John Hill, Richard Claridge. Acknowledged Aug 15 1722 before Jacob Loockerman and assoc. Justices. G. Loockerman, Clk.

2 Old 134/Aug 10 1722/Thomas White, Carpenter, and Elizabeth his wife to John Young: Part of "Mill Point," "in a Marsh on ye west side of Transquakin River usually called Beckwiths Island," containing 16 a. more or less. Wit: Ar. Smith, Jno Cullen. Acknowledged Aug 16 1722 before Jacob Loockerman and assoc. Justices. G. Loockerman, Clk.

2 Old 135/Apr 3 1722/William Evans, Sarah Evans and Daniel Ryan to Henry Ennalls: Upper half of "Humphries Fortune" at head of Fishing Creek, containing 200 a. more or less. Wit: Charles Ungle, William Murray. Acknowledged Apr 3 1722 before Henry Ennalls and John Rider, Justices.

2 Old 136/Jul 18 1722/Edward Billiter and Ann his wife to John Tomlinson: 100 a., part of "Nancies Delight" on W. side of NW Branch of Nanticoke River. Wit: Joseph Allford, Mark Fisher. Acknowledged Aug 15 1722 before Jacob Loockerman assos. Justices. G. Loockerman, Clk.

2 Old 137/Aug 6 1722/William Scotten and Mary his wife to James Anderton: Part of "Widow's Purchase," containing 250 a. more or less. Wit: Henry Hooper, John Davis. Acknowledged Aug 17 1722 before Jacob Loockerman and assoc. Justices. G. Loockerman, Clk.

2 Old 138/Jun 4 1722/Betty Caco, Queen of Ababco Indians, and Pemetasusk, Queen of the Hard Swamp Indians, with other Indians, to William Murray: Land at head of Blackwater, adj land of John Trivallion and containing 70 a. more or less. Wit: Thomas Ennalls, William Spincer. Acknowledged Jun 4 1722 before Henry Ennalls and Peter Taylor, Justices.

2 Old 139/Dec 13 1706/Thomas Billingsley and Sarah Billingsley, otherwise known as Sarah Hance, now the wife of John Hance, all of Calvert County, to William Smith of Dorchester County: "Billingsley's Chance" on Chicamocomico or Phillips Creek, containing 300 a. more or less. Wit: Thomas Ennalls, William Fookes. Acknowledged Mar 16 1722 by Henry Ennalls, Atty for Thomas Billingsley and Hannah his wife, John Hance and Sarah his wife, before Joseph Ennalls and Francis Hayward, Justices, by virtue of Power of Atty dated Dec 9 1706.

2 Old 140/Jul 7 1719/Survey and plat of "Maulden" on Cooks Point for Capt. Henry Trippe and Edward Cook, by Hodson, Surveyor.

2 Old 140/nov 14 1722/Sarah Webb to Lamrock Flowers: "Phillips Range" on Phillips Creek, containing 200 a. more or less. Wit: Joseph Kennerly, John Stevens, Joseph Wray. Acknowledged Nov 14 1722 before Roger Woolford, Justice.

2 Old 141/Nov 15 1722/John Kirke to John White: Uppermost part of "Newport" on Blackwater River and Hocketty Creek or branch, containing 80 a., adj "Hocketty." Acknowledged Nov 15 1722 by John Kirke and Sarah his wife, before Jacob Loockerman and assoc. Justices. G. Loockerman, Clk.

2 Old 142/Nov 14 1722/John White to Thomas White: Part of "The Plains" in Hunting Creek containing 150 a. more or less. Wit: L. Flowers, John Stephens,

Joseph Kennarley. Acknowledged Nov 14 1722 before Roger Woolford, Justice.

2 Old 143/Nov 15 1722/Francis Allen and Mary his wife to John Eccleston: All their right of "Dower, Title, Interest, Claim and Demand" in lands owned by Hugh Eccleston Junr. at the time of his death. Wit: Jacob Loockerman, Richard Webster. Acknowledged Nov 15 1722 before Jacob Loockerman and assoc. Justices. G. Loockerman, Clk.

2 Old 143/Aug 3 1722/Mary Harper, Andrew Goutee and Agnes Goutee his wife to William Shenton: Part of "Skillington's" lying between John Harper's and Ramon Shenton's. Acknowledged Sep 8 1722 before John Keene and John Robson, Justices.

2 Old 144/Dec 9 1706/Thomas Billingsley and Hannah his wife, John Hance and Sarah his wife to Henry Ennalls: Power of Atty to convey "Billingsley's Chance" to William Smith of Dorchester County. Wit: Robert Don, Thomas Cullingburrow, Thomas Allderson. Proved Dec 11 1706 by Robert Don and Thomas Cullingburrow, before Joseph Ennalls, Justice.

2 Old 145/Nov 1722/Henry Hooper to William Ennalls: First Lot in Vienna, containing 3/4 a. Wit: John Davis, Thomas Smith. Acknowledged Nov 16 1722 before Jacob Loockerman and assoc. Justices. G. Loockerman, Clk.

2 Old 145/Nov 10 1722/Richard Woodland, Planter, and Johannah his wife to Henry Lake, Junr., Blacksmith: Part of "Betty's Chance" adj "Musketta Neck" on Hungar River, containing 55 a. more or less. Wit: William Edgar, Michael Todd. Acknowledged Nov 16 1722 by William Evans, Atty for grantors, before Jacob Loockerman and assoc. Justices. G. Loockerman, Clk.

2 Old 147/Nov 14 1722/Lamarock Flowers and Patience his wife to Thomas White: Two parcels of land on W. side of Transquakin River, first lot being 1/2 of "Anderson's Neck" originally granted to John Anderson for 300 a. by patent dated Aug 18 1665, and the second lot being 1/2 of "Anderson's Neck Regulated," adj land of William Whayland and containing 107 a. more or less. Wit: Joseph Kennarley, John Stevens, John White. Acknowledged Nov 14 1722 before Roger Woolford, Justice.

2 Old 148/Jan 15 1722/John Harwood and Rebecca his wife to their children Thomas Brannock, Ann Brannock and Rachell Brannock: Personalty.

2 Old 148/Jan 26 1722/Joseph MacCloster (Maclester, MacClester) and Isabell his wife of Somerset County to Marcus Andrews of Dorchester County: "Racoon Point" on S. side of Racoon Creek which issues out of Blackwater River, containing 244 a. Wit: James Hayes, John Rider. Acknowledged Jan 28 1722 before John Rider and Thomas Taylor, Justices.

2 Old 149/Jan 22 1722/3/Elizabeth Colloe, widow, to her daughter Hannah (Haner) Alford: "Poines Point" on N. side of Hog Creek, containing 250 a. more or less. Wit: John Sharp, Benjamin Nicolls. Acknowledged Feb 11 1722 by William Chipley, Atty for grantor before Henry Trippe and Thomas Taylor, Justices.

2 Old 151/Mar 12 1722/Joseph Woodward and Mary his wife to Henry Trippe: "Bintree," containing 50 a. on a branch of Blackwater River; and "Aye," containing 17 a. on a branch of Blackwater River. Wit: Isaac Nicolls, David Fowler. Acknowledged May 15 1722 before Henry Ennalls and John Robson, Justices.

2 Old 152/Mar 13 1722/Robert Dickenson, son and heir of Walter Dickenson late of Kent County, Delaware, deceased, to Samuel Dickenson of Talbot County:

"Holborn" containing 1000 a.; "Mount Andrew" containing 300 a.; and "Plow Yard" containing 200 a. Wit: Thomas Baynard, James Pemberton, Peter Sharp. Acknowledged Mar 13 1722 before Jacob Loockerman and assoc. Justices. G. Loockerman, Clk.

2 Old 153/Jun 6 1723/John Robson to his sons John Robson and Roger Robson: Grantor's dwelling plantation and other land in the neck called "Widow's Neck," at death of grantor. Wit: J. Davis, Thomas Woolford. Acknowledged Jun 6 1723 before Roger Woolford, Justice.

2 Old 153/1706-1709/Testimony of Philip Shapleigh of Northumberland County, Virginia, aged 61 years or thereabouts, formerly Deputy Surveyor of Dorchester County, re bounds of "Philipsburgh" surveyed in 1670 for Philip Calvert on Transquakin, then called Chicamocomico or Philips Creek, near land of Richard Mears. Testimony of Henry Hooper, aged about 63 years, re bounds of "Philipsburgh" Testimony of William Smith aged about 43 years re bounds of "Philipsburgh"

2 Old 154/Oct 5 1687/Richard Bradley to Bartholomew Ennalls: "Bradley's Adventure" on Transquakin River, adj land of John Pierson and containing 60 a. more or less, granted to Henry Bradley deceased. Wit: John Brook, Henry Howard, Obediah King. Acknowledged Oct 8 1687 before John Brooke and Charles Hutchins.

2 Old 155/May 10 1723/George Stapleforte to John Griffin: "Bull Point." Wit: John Griffin Junr., George Griffin. Acknowledged Jun 10 1723 before Jacob Loockerman and assoc. Justices. G. Loockerman, Clk.

2 Old 156/Jul 8 1723/George Plater of Calvert County to William Ennalls, Merchant of Dorchester County: "Darby" on E. side of Blackwater River and Hockady's Creek, containing 500 a. more or less. Wit: Samuel Young, John Lawson. Acknowledged Jul 8 1723 before Samuel Young, Chief Justice of the Provincial Court of Maryland.

2 Old 157/Mar 1722/3/John Eccleston to his brother Thomas Eccleston: Several contiguous tracts between Gary's Creek and Arthur Wright's Creek. Wit: John LeCompte, Bazell Noell. Acknowledged Mar 15 1722 before Jacob Loockerman and assoc. Justices. G. Loockerman, Clk.

2 Old 158/Jun 12 1723/William Edmondson, Merchant, to Solomon Edmondson, Carpenter: Part of "Richardson's Folly" containing 165 a. more or less. Wit: Michael Fletcher, Charles Ungle. Acknowledged Jun 12 1723 before Jacob Loockerman and assoc. Justices. G. Loockerman, Clk.

2 Old 158/Apr 27 1723/John Lane and John Willson of Queen Annes County to Thomas Hampson of Talbot County: "Lanes Chance" near the head of Great Choptank River containing 100 a. more or less according to survey of James Hayes, Surveyor, dated May 7 1720. Wit: Will. Gough, Phinehas Willson. Acknowledged Jun 4 1723 before Robert Goldsborough and assoc. Justices. Phil Feddeman, Clk for Talbot County.

2 Old 159/Feb 6 1706/Receipt for 18 buck skins and one bed tick from Joshua Morgan for use of William Dixon of Talbot County, Glover, received at New Castle upon Delaware by John Richeson Sr. Wit: Silvester Garland.

2 Old 159/Mar 14 1722/Peter Taylor and Mary Taylor his wife to Ann Turbutt, Spinster: "Goose Pond" on a branch of Nanticoke, containing 200 a. more or less. Wit: J. Davis, Richard Webster, Nico. Lowe. Acknowledged Mar 14 1722 before Jacob Loockerman and assoc. Justices. G. Loockerman, Clk.

2 Old 161/Mar 13 1722/Thomas Hayward to Henry Ennalls: Land devised to grant-
or by the Last Will and Testament of Col. Thomas Ennalls deceased, at head of
Shoal Creek where Andrew Willis lived, adj land where William Jones lived;
part of "Ennalls Purchase," containing 50 a. more or less. Wit: G. Loockerman, Bar. Ennalls. Acknowledged Mar 13 1722 before Jacob Loockerman and
assoc. Justices. G. Loockerman, Clk.

2 Old 161/Mar 15 1722/John Eccleston, Mariner, to Thomas Eccleston, Planter:
"Edmondson's Ridge" in the freshes of Great Choptank River, containing 400 a.
more or less. Wit: John LeCompte, Bazell Noell. Acknowledged Mar 15 1722
before Jacob Loockerman and assoc. Justices. G. Loockerman, Clk.

2 Old 162/Feb 18 1722/Henry Trippe to William Paine: 100 a., part of "Trippes
Horse Range" near head of Hunting Creek. Wit: Phil Feddeman, Fra. Anderton.
Acknowledged Mar 14 1722 by Henry Trippe and Susannah his wife, before Roger
Woolford, Justice.

2 Old 163/Jul 13 1722/George Hooper to James Insley: Part of "Andrews Fortune"
formerly belonging to Andrew Insley and given by him to his daughter Mary
Insley, who later became the mother of said George Hooper; said parcel of
land commonly called the "Road Ridge," adj "Betty's Lott" and containing 50 a.
more or less. Acknowledged Jul 14 1722 by George Hooper and Michael Todd,
Atty for Silvia Hooper, wife of George Hooper, before John Keene and John
Robson, Justices.

2 Old 164/Mar 15 1722/Nathaniel Smith and Margaret his wife to Rebecca
Charlescraft, Spinster: 100 a. being 1/2 of "Cumberland." Wit: Anthony
Rawlings, John Pitt. Acknowledged Mar 15 1722 before Jacob Loockerman and
assoc. Justices. G. Loockerman, Clk.

2 Old 165/Mar 11 1722/Release of Goovert Loockerman from Elizabeth Watson,
Relict of William Watson, deceased. Wit: P. Eilbeck, Sarah Loockerman.

2 Old 165/Mar 11 1722/Release of Elizabeth Watson, Relict of William Watson,
deceased, from G. Loockerman. Wit: P. Eilbeck, Sarah Loockerman.

2 Old 165/Bill of Exchange for Eleven Pounds Sterling, drawn on Thomas Davis
of England, by his brother, Henry Davis. Margaret Davis, wife of Thomas
Davis.

2 Old 165/Feb 10 1723/George Staplefort and Jane Staplefort his wife to
William Robson: "Staplefort's Chance" on E. side of Blackwater River, con-
taining 27 a. more or less. Wit: Thomas Taylor, William Smith, J. Davis.
Acknowledged Mar 13 1722 before Jacob Loockerman and assoc. Justices by
George Staplefort and Thomas Taylor, Atty for Jane Staplefort. G. Loocker-
man, Clk.

2 Old 167/Mar 15 1722/Edward Billiter to Peter Taylor: "Fancy," on a branch
of Philips Creek, adj "Doncaster" and "Edmondson's Reserve" and containing
100 a. Wit: Thomas Eccleston, Richard Webster. Acknowledged Mar 13 1722
before Jacob Loockerman and assoc. Justices. G. Loockerman, Clk.

2 Old 167/1722/Matthew Harmanson of North Hampton County, Virginia, and
Easter his wife to William Polk of Dorchester County: "Collier's Adventure"
containing 250 a. more or less, formerly patented to Robert Collier late of
Somerset County deceased by deed of grant dated 1674, conveyed by said
Collier to Henry Matthews of North Hampton County, Virginia, conveyed by said
Matthews to Matthew Patrick of Virginia, and devised by said Patrick to his
grandson, Matthew Harmanson, by his Last Will and Testament. Wit: James

Polak (Polk), James Bruksher. Acknowledged Dec 11 by John Pollett, atty for
Matthew Harmanson and Easter his wife, before John Rider and Charles Nutter.

2 Old 169/Dec 11 1722/Richard Layton to James Polk (Pollok) of Somerset
County: "Dublin" containing 100 a. more or less, formerly granted to John
Clayburn of Dorchester County by patent dated May 21 1696, conveyed by Wm
Williams and Mary his wife and Thomas Williams and Anna his wife, heirs of
said John Clayburn, to Richard Layton. Wit: Thomas Smith, John Pollet.
Acknowledged Dec 11 before John Rider and Charles Nutter.

2 Old 170/mar 13 1722/Thomas Hunt and Anne his wife to Patrick Broughan:
"Hogg Island" on a branch of Blackwater, containing 53 a. more or less.
Acknowledged Mar 13 1722/3 before Jacob Loockerman and John Robinson,
Justices.

2 Old 171/Jul 7 1723/Thomas Wilson of Kent County, Pennsylvania to Abraham
Covington of Dorchester County: "Poplar Island" containing 100 a. more or
less, in Fishing Bay. Wit: James Cannon, William Clarkson. Acknowledged
Jul 28 1723 before John Rider and Charles Nutter, Justices.

2 Old 172/Aug 14 1723/William Cheattell to Samuel Dickinson: "Hamstead" adj
"Kirkman's Discovery" on Watts Creek and containing 600 a. more or less.
Wit: Charles Ungle, J. Davis, John Gorsuch. Acknowledged Aug 14 1723 before
Jacob Loockerman and assoc. Justices. G. Loockerman, Clk.

2 Old 173/Aug 14 1723/Joshua Morgan to William Ennalls: "Wales" on a branch
of the NW fork of Nanticoke, containing 50 a. more or less. Wit: John
Eccleston, Francis Hayward Jr. Acknowledged Aug 14 1723 before Jacob
Loockerman and assoc. Justices. G. Loockerman, Clk.

2 Old 174/Aug 14 1723/James Holland to Hezekiah Vickery: "Pleasant," taken up
by Henry Davis and assigned by him to James Holland. Wit: Richard Webster,
Benony Frazier. Acknowledged Aug 14 1723 before Jacob Loockerman and assoc.
Justices. G. Loockerman, Clk.

2 Old 175/1723/William Clayton and Katherine his wife to John Standford: Part
of "London" on the E. side of Blackwater River, adj "Hocaty" and "West Town,"
and containing 140 a. more or less. Wit: Evan Evans, William Pieary.
Acknowledged Aug 8 1723 before Nicholas Goldsborough and Daniel Sherwood,
Justices for Talbot County. Phill. Feddeman, Clk.

3 Old 1/May 28 1673/William Killman of James Island, planter to Robert Sikes late of Somerset County, planter: "Kollman's Range" containing 100 a. on an island adj land formerly laid out for Francis Armstrong and now in the possession of said Killman. Wit: Edward Cooke, Edward Savage. Acknowledged Jun 3 1673. Edward Sauvage, Clk.

3 Old 2/Jun 24 1671 - Nov 25 1671/Thomas Thurston of Balt County to Thomas Hooker: 350 a. on Great Choptank River. Wit: John Hillen, Richard Arnold. Acknowledged by John Edmondson of Talbot County, Atty for grantor, Jun 3 1673. Edward Sauvage, Clk. Power of Atty witnessed by Owen Griffith, Charles Bardon.

3 Old 2/Mar 5 1673/Thomas Hooker of Ann Arundel to John Willson: Land formerly assigned to Hooker by Thomas Thurston. Wit: John Hillen, Nathaniell Hillen. Acknowledged Jun 3 1673 in open Court by Peter Baucomb, Atty for Thomas Hooker. Edward Sauvage, Clk.

3 Old 3/Mar 14 1669/John Edmondson of Talbot County, Merchant to William Canon (Canning) of Bristol, Merchant: Part of "Richeson's Folly" on Skillington's Creek adj Thomas Skillington's land and containing 500 a. more or less. Wit: Thomas Skillington, Peter Baucomb. Assigned by William Canning to John Edmondson Jun 2 1673. Wit: Daniell Clark, R. Turner. Acknowledged Jun 3 1673 by William Canning. Edward Sauvage, Clk.

3 Old 4/Dec 26 1672/Henry Turner and Henry Parker of Dorchester County to John Brooke of said County, Chirurgeon: "Partnership" at the head of Blackwater adj land formerly laid out for Isaac Abrams called "Ashbourn," and containing 200 a. more or less. Wit: Rd. Rayner, Sheldon Berry. Acknowledged Aug 5 1673 by Grantors. Edward Sauvage, Clk.

3 Old 5/Aug 2 1670/Thomas Hooton of Dorchester County, Planter to Isaac Hunt of Dorchester County, Planter: "Hooton's Neck" on Hungar River containing 50 a. more or less. Wit: Thomas Skinner, James Selby. Acknowledged Aug 2 1670 in open Court. Edward Sauvage, Clk.

3 Old 6/Aug 5 1673/Bond of Thomas Taylor, "new High Sherr. of the said County" to Samuel Millington re "Hooton's Neck" sold by Thomas Hooton to Isaac Hunt. Wit: William Wroughton, Thomas Pattison. Acknowledged Aug 5 1673. Edward Sauvage, Clk.

3 Old 7/Jun 1 1673/Bond of Thomas Oliver of Dorchester County, Boatwright, to William Killman of Dorchester County, Planter, re sale of 200 a. called "Long Point" made between William Killman on the one part and Thomas Oliver and Lawrence Simmons on the other part. Wit: William Merchant Jr, Edward Sauvage. Acknowledged Aug 5 1673 in open Court. Edward Sauvage, Clk.

3 Old 7/Apr 23 1673/John Edmondson of Talbot County, Gent. to John Richardson of the same county, Planter: "Fox Hill" containing 200 a. on Marshy Creek adj land of George Richardson; and "Skipton" containing 200 a. at the head of Fox Creek. Sarah, wife of John Edmondson. Wit: John Standley, Edward Williams. Acknowledged Aug 5 1673. Edward Sauvage, Clk.

3 Old 8/Feb 26 1661/John Clements of Talbot County, Merchant from John Pitt and Frances his wife of Talbot County, Merchant: "Stockaday" in Dorchester County on Blackwater. Acknowledged Mar 5 1673. Edward Sauvage, Clk.

3 Old 9/Aug 5 1673/John Edmondson of Talbot County, Gent. and James Morphey of the county afsd to Thomas Taylor of Dorchester County, Gent.: "Request" on

NE branch of Transquakin River, containing 300 a. Sarah, wife of John
Edmondson; Mary, wife of James Morphey. Wit: John Ingram, Henry Turner.
Acknowledged Mar 5 1673. Edward Sauvage, Clk.

3 Old 10/Aug 5 1673/James Murphey of Talbot County, Planter to Thomas Taylor
of Dorchester County, Gent.: 500 a. on Transquakin River in the occupation of
Murphey. Mary, wife of James Murphey. Wit: John Ingram, Henry Turner.
Acknowledged Aug 5 1673. Edward Sauvage, Clk.

3 Old 12/Jun 24 1671/Thomas Thurston of Baltimore County to Thomas Hooker of
Ann Arundel County: "Elberton's" on Watts Creek on the NE branch of Great
Choptank River, containing 350 a. more or less, part of a tract formerly
granted to George Richardson by patent. Wit: John Hillen. Acknowledged Aug
5 1673 by John Edmondson, Atty for Grantor. Edward Sauvage, Clk.

3 Old 13/Mar 25 1673/Thomas Hooker of Ann Arundel County to John Willson of
the afsd County: "Elberton's" formerly conveyed to Hooker by Thomas Thurston,
containing 350 a. more or less. Wit: J. Hillen, Nathaniell Hillen. Acknowledged Sep 2 1673 by Peter Baucomb, Atty for Grantor. Edward Sauvage, Clk.

3 Old 15/Jun 26 1673/John Briggs of Dorchester County, to Thomas Hooker of
Ann Arundel County, Planter: "Parthomell," "Lying in the County of Dorchester
aforesaid on the South Side of Greatt Choptank River Some two miles below
the devideing of the River" and containing 100 a. more or less. Also
"Parthomas," containing 50 a. more or less. Wit: Edward Lacy, Henry Steven-
son. Acknowledged Sep 2 1673 by Peter Baucomb, Atty for Grantor. Edward
Sauvage, Clk.

3 Old 17/Feb 14 1672/Richard Gibbs of Pearcheam in England, Merchant, to
William Brett of Dorchester County, Merchant: Part of "Armstrong's Folly"
containing 200 a. by estimation. Wit: Thomas Pattison, Edward Sauvage, A.
Wright. Acknowledged Sep 2 1673 to Arthur Wright, Atty for William Brett.
Edward Sauvage, Clk.

3 Old 18/Nov 4 1673/William Brett of St. James Island in Dorchester County,
Planter, to John Evans: Part of "Goodridges Choice" adj land of Andrew Gray
and containing 200 a. Wit: A. Wright, Ralph Powell. Acknowledged Nov 4 1673.
Edward Sauvage, Clk.

3 Old 20/Nov 4 1672/William Willowby of Dorchester County, "Playsterer" and
John Stratton of Dorchester County, Planter, to William Fisher: "Raxall" adj
land of Anthony LeCompte and containing 50 a. Hannah, wife of William
Willowby. Wit: Robert Staplefort, John Bloare. Acknowledged Nov 5 1672 by
grantors. Edward Sauvage, Clk. Assigned by William Fisher to William
Willowby Nov 4 1673. Wit: Andrew Price, Gourney Crowe. Acknowledged Nov 4
1673 by William Fisher to William Willowby. Edward Sauvage, Clk.

3 Old 21/Sep 3 1673/John Whinfield of Calvert County, Planter, to John
Pollard of Dorchester County, Wine Cooper: "Whinfell" containing 200 a. more
or less, on Chesapeake Bay behind St. James Point and on Back Creek, patented
to Whinfield Mar 8 1666. Wit: Thomas Newman, Benjamin Granger, John Hungerford, William Watkins, Francis Twyford. Acknowledged Nov 4 1673. Edward
Sauvage, Clk.

3 Old 22/Nov 2 1671/John Edmondson to George Prowse of Dorchester County,
Planter: 1/2 of "Britt's Hope" on Smiths Creek, containing 600 a. more or
less. Signed by John Edmondson and John Holt (Hoult) making void all former
bills of sale from Edmondson to Holt for this land. Wit: Robert Evans,
Thomas Skillington. Acknowledged Nov 4 1673. Edward Sauvage, Clk. Agree-

ment between George Prowse and Andrew Perdo re division of "Brett's Hope" purchased by them from John Edmondson. Dated Feb 17 1672 and witnessed by Anthony Mayl, John Holt.

3 Old 24/Nov 1 1673/John Edmondson to William Jones, Master and mariner of Bristol: Land on N. side of Philip's Creek containing 800 a. more or less. Wit: Ri. Gorsuch, William Brett. Acknowledged Nov 4 1673 to Edward Roe, Atty for William Jones. Edward Sauvage, Clk.

3 Old 25/Nov 3 1673/John Rawlings, Boatwright of Dorchester County to his "father in law" Michaell Basey of Dorchester County: 100 a. for the lifetime of Basey and the lifetime or widowhood of his wife, Joanna Basey, mother of said John Rawlings. Wit: John Brooke, Henry Brooke. Acknowledged Nov 4 1673. Edward Sauvage, Clk.

3 Old 25/Dec 1 1673/John Brooke of Dorchester County, Chirurgeon to Francis Tassell of Dorchester County, Planter: Land called "Partnership" (?) on S. side of Little Choptank at the head of Blackwater adj land laid out for Isaac Abrahams called "Ashbourne" and containing 200 a. more or less. Wit: E... B..., Henry Turner. Acknowledged Dec 2 1673. Edward Sauvage, Clk.

3 Old 26/Nov 4 1673/Henry Mitchell of Calvert County, Planter to William Stevens of Dorchester County, Gent.: "Ceader Poynt" containing 150 a. more or less. Wit: William Brett, John Holt. Acknowledged first Tuesday in Nov 1673. Edward Sauvage, Clk. Bond witnessed by William Brett, Thomas Taylor.

3 Old 28/Nov 5 1673/Ralph Powell of Dorchester County, Planter to Thomas Taylor of the same County, Planter: 100 a., 1/2 of a tract of land on Cabin Creek called "Addition," formerly in the occupation of John Richardson. Acknowledged Nov 9 1673. Edward Sauvage, Clk. Bond witnessed by Arthur Wright, William Jones.

3 Old 30/Dec 2 1713(1673?)/John Kirke of Dorchester County, Planter to John Stevens of the same County, Boatwright: "Poplar Plaines" on Blackwater River, adj land of William Dorrington and containing 200 a. more or less. Alce, wife of John Kirke. Wit: A. Wright, John Darby, William Willowby, Francis Tassell. Acknowledged Jan 6 1673. Edward Sauvage, Clk.

3 Old 31/Jan 6 1673/Thomas Oliver of Dorchester County, Planter to Samuell Pritchett of said County, Planter: Part of "Humphreys Fortune" on a branch of Fishing Creek. Susan, wife of Thomas Oliver. Wit: Henry Aldred, John Edwards, Thomas Pattison. Acknowledged Jan 6 1673. Edward Sauvage, Clk.

3 Old 33/On the back of deed from William Killman to Robert Sykes for 100 a. called "Killman's Range": Assignment of said "Killman's Range" from Robert Sykes to Thomas Pattison. Acknowledged Jan 6 1673.

3 Old 33/Jan 5 1673/Robert Sykes of Dorchester County, Cooper to Thomas Pattison of the same County, Gent.: "Killman's Range" on James Island adj land laid out for Francis Armstrong and containing 100 a. more or less. Wit: William Coursey, Peter Sayer. Acknowledged Jan 6 1673. Edward Sauvage, Clk.

3 Old 34/Jan 6 1673/James Williams of Calvert County, Planter, and Mary his wife to Richard Owen of Dorchester County, Planter: "John's Garden" on Todds Bay adj land formerly owned by John Edmondson and containing 200 a. more or less. Wit: Richard Rainer, Anthony Dawson. Acknowledged Jan 6 1673 by John Brooke, Atty for grantors. Edward Sauvage, Clk. Power of Atty witnessed by Richard Hartheny, Daniell Robeson.

3 Old 36/Nov 9 1673/Thomas Broxome of Dorchester County, Planter to Robert
Sykes of said county, Planter: "Hooton's Folly" on an island, called Hoops
and Chapleys Island, on Hungar River and containing 50 a. more or less. Wit:
A. Wright, Edward Sauvage. Acknowledged Jan 6 1673. Edward Sauvage, Clk.

3 Old 37/Dec 5 1671//Thomas Newton of Dorchester County, Planter to Francis
Twyford of the same County, Planter: "Georges Choyce" at the head of Salt
Marsh Creek of Little Choptank River, containing 100 a. more or less. Sarah,
wife of Thomas Newton. Wit: A. Wright, Thomas Ashley. Acknowledged Dec 5
1671. Edward Sauvage, Clk. Assignment of above land from Francis Twyford to
William Jones. Witnessed by Edward Sauvage and Morris Matthews. Acknowledged Jan 6 1673. Edward Sauvage, Clk.

3 Old 39/Mar 3 1673/John Edmondson of Dorchester County, Merchant to Peter
Baucomb of the same County, Chirurgeon: "Hope Poynt," part of a tract of 300
a., 200 a. having been sold to Robert Francis and the remaining 100 a. being
conveyed herein to said Baucomb. Wit: Thomas Taylor, Thomas Vaughan.
Acknowledged in open Court Mar 3 1673. Edward Sauvage, Clk.

3 Old 40/Jun 1 1674/Arthur Wright, Planter to James Brown, Planter: "Five
Pines" on Castle Haven Bay, containing 106 a. more or less. Abigaill, wife
of Arthur Wright. Wit: Edward Sauvage, Thomas Gilbert. Acknowledged the
second Tuesday of Jun 1674 before Robert Winsmore and Bartholomew Ennalls,
Justices. Edward Sauvage, Clk.

3 Old 41/Jul 15 1674/Thomas Newton of Dorchester County, Planter to Edward
Sauvage of the same place, Clerk: "Daniells Pasture" on Little Choptank River
adj land where Daniell Clarke lives and containing 100 a. more or less.
Sarah, wife of Thomas Newton. Wit: Robert Dix; Thomas Seamans. Acknowledged
Aug 4 1674. Edward Sauvage, Clk.

3 Old 43/Jul 15 1674/Edward Sauvage of Dorchester County to Morrice Mathews
of the same place, Planter: "Daniells Pasture." Wit: John Alford. Acknowledged Aug 4 1674. Edward Sauvage, Clk. Bond witnessed by John Alford, John
Mackeel.

3 Old 44/Jul 8 1674/Henry Turner of Dorchester County, Gent. to James Agg of
the same place, cordwainer and William Merchant, Planter: "Ipswich" on Blackwater River containing 132 a. more or less. Wit: Francis Tassell, Joseph
Serjant. Acknowledged Aug 4 1674 in open Court. Edward Sauvage. Clk.

3 Old 45/Aug 4 1674/George Cooley, Planter to Francis Billingsley of the
Clifts in Calvert County, Planter: "Cleeland" in the freshes of Hogg Creek
containing 250 a. more or less. Wit: John Brooke, Giles Blyzard (Blizard).
Acknowledged Aug 4 1674 to Thomas Skillington, Atty for Francis Billingsley.
Edward Sauvage, Clk. Power of Atty witnessed by Thomas Wilkinson, James
Wilkinson.

3 Old 47/Jun 8 1674/John Richardson of Dorchester County, Planter to Andrew
Gray of Dorchester County, Planter: "Goodridges Choice" on Cabin Creek con-
taining 600 a. more or less. Susannah, wife of John Richardson. Wit:
William Wattson, George Watts. Acknowledged Aug 4 1674. Edward Sauvage,
Clk. Bond witnessed by William Wattson, Thomas Flowers, George Watts.

3 Old 49/Jul 26 1673/Katherine Phillips to her husband, John Phillips: All
her property. Wit: Richard Tubman, Robert Freeland, John Reenly. Acknowledged Aug 4 1674. Edward Sauvage, Clk.

3 Old 50/Jul 18 1674/John Richardson of Dorchester County, planter, and
Susanna his wife, to Simon Richardson and John Yeale (Yale) of the same

County, planters: "Goodridge's Choice" on Cabin Creek adj land of Timothy Goodridge and containing 300 a. more or less. Wit: Thomas Morris, William Chesum, Cornelius Haley. Acknowledged Aug 4 1674. Edward Sauvage, Clk.

3 Old 51/Nov 28 1673/Robert Blinkhorne, Planter of St. Leonard's Creek in Patuxent River in Calvert County to Richard Tubman of Dorchester County, Planter: "Mathews Vinyard" containing 100 a., granted to said Blinkhorne by patent dated Sep 10 1666, adj land laid out for John Felton on Limbo River. Wit: Andrew Insley, Thomas Brown. Acknowledged Aug 4 1674 by John Phillips, Atty for said Robert and Bridgett his wife. Edward Sauvage, Clk.

3 Old 54/Mar 6 1673/Obadiah Judkin of Talbot County, Boatwright to Miles Mason late of the Clifts in Patuxent River, Planter: 1/2 of Tewton on Little Choptank River and Fishing Creek, containing 250 a. more or less. Wit: John Darby, Edward Sauvage. Acknowledged Sep 1 1674. Edward Sauvage, Clk.

3 Old 55/Aug 29 1674/William Worgin of Dorchester County, Planter to Edward Sauvage, Gent.: "All that one moyety of a parcel of Land called 'Worgins Chance' heretofore given to the said County of Dorchester afsd to Build a Court House thereupon" containing 50 a. of land, moyety containing 25 a. Wit: Owen Murphy, Thomas Gilbert. Acknowledged Sep 1 1674. Edward Sauvage, Clk.

3 Old 57/Oct 6 1674/William Jones of Dorchester County, planter to William Ford of the same place Gent.: "Hereford" on Blackwater Creek containing 550 a. Jane (Jone?), wife of William Jones. Wit: John Rawlings, Henry Turner. Acknowledged Oct 6 1674. Edward Sauvage, Clk.

3 Old 59/Oct 4 1674/John Rawlings and Philadelphia his wife of Dorchester County, Boatwright, to William Merchant of the same County, Planter: "Merchants Adventure" on Transquakin River containing 150 a. more or less. Wit: Thyin McNamara, Thomas Newman. Acknowledged Oct 6 1673. Edward Sauvage, Clk.

3 Old 60/Sep 20 1674/John Rawlings and Philadelphia his wife of Dorchester County, Boatwright to Thomas Sewell of the same County, Planter: "Sewell's Choyce" on Transquakin River, containing 100 a. more or less. Wit: Gournay Crowe, John Wigfield. Acknowledged Oct 6 1674. Edward Sauvage, Clk.

3 Old 61/Sep 16 1674/John Rawlings and Philadelphia his wife of Dorchester County, Boatwright to James Peterkin of Dorchester County, Mariner: "Plaine Dealling" on Trsnquakin River, adj "Partnership" and containing 200 a. more or less. Wit: Peter Underwood, William Jones. Acknowledged Oct 6 1674. Edward Sauvage, Clk.

3 Old 62/Aug 29 1674/James Jones of Somerset County, Planter to Charles Hutchings, Carpenter of Dorchester County: Land on Nanticoke River containing 300 a., called "Goodings Adventure." Sarah, wife of James Jones. Acknowledged Oct 6 1674. Edward Sauvage, Clk. Bond witnessed by Henry Parker, John Phillips.

3 Old 64/Oct 7 1674/William Willowby of Dorchester County, "Plaisterer" to Thomas Pattison of the same County, Wine Cooper: "Exchange" on a branch of Transquakin River. Hannah, wife of William Willoby. Wit: William Stephens, Thomas Newman. Acknowledged Oct 6 1674. Edward Sauvage, Clk.

3 Old 65/Sep 22 1674/John Brooke of Dorchester County, Chyrurgeon and Planter to Humphrey Hubbart of the same county, Cooper: 200 a. more or less called "Hasellwood" on a branch of Transquakin River adj land of Thomas Taylor. Wit: William Dossey, William Berry. Acknowledged Oct 6 1674. Edward Sauvage, Clk.

3 Old 66/Oct 6 1674/Henry Parker of Talbot County, Gent. to Henry Bradley of Dorchester County, Planter: "Parker's Chance" on Transquakin River, containing 500 a. Wit: A. Wright, Gourney Crow. Acknowledged Oct 6 1674. Edward Sauvage, Clk.

3 Old 68/The last day of August, 1674/Henry Turner of Dorchester County, Carpenter, to Thomas Vicars of the same county, Planter: "Clarridge" near the head of a branch of Fishing Creek in Little Choptank River called Tewdon, containing 100 a. more or less. Abigaill, wife of Henry Turner. Wit: Thomas Wall, John Dossey. Acknowledged Oct 6 1674. Edward Sauvage, Clk.

3 Old 69/Nov 2 1674/Anthony Hardacre of Dorchester County, Planter to Peter Stoakes of the same place, Planter: Part of "Hayles Choyce" on a branch of Fishing Creek on the S. side of Little Choptank River, containing 100 a. more or less, 50 a. being conveyed. Wit: Thomas Gilbert, Edward Sauvage. Acknowledged Nov 3 1674. Edward Sauvage, Clk.

3 Old 71/Nov 3 1674/Thomas Wall of Dorchester County, Planter to William Worgin and Alice his wife of the same County, Inholder: 100 a. called "Snake Poynt" on Fishing Creek and Little Choptank River. Wit: Ri. Gorsuch, Ralph Wells, Gournay Crow. Acknowledged Nov 3 1674. Edward Sauvage, Clk.

3 Old 72/Dec 1 1674/John Clements of Talbot County, Gent. to William Ford of Dorchester County, Gent.: "Hockady" containing 600 a. by estimation in Blackwater. Mary, wife of John Clements. Wit: Henry Trippe, Thomas Taylor. Acknowledged Dec 1 1674. Edward Sauvage, Clk.

3 Old 74/Nov 2 1674/Nicholas Hackett of Talbot County, Planter to William Jones of Bristol England, Mariner: "St. Jones" on Phillips Creek containing 500 a. more or less, adj land laid out for John Edmondson called "Dorchester." Wit: Geo. Cowley, Ri. Gorsuch. Acknowledged Nov 3 1674. Edward Sauvage, Clk.

3 Old 75/Aug 11 1674/George Cowley (Cooley) of Talbot County to Thomas Lambert of London, England, Merchant: "Derby" on Blackwater, containing 400 a. more or less. Wit: Richard Gorsuch, Robert Staplefort, Howell Powell. Acknowledged Nov 3 1674. Edward Sauvage, Clk.

3 Old 77/Nov 12 1674/John Richardson of Dorchester County, Planter to Jacob Seth of the same County: Part of "Huntingfield" containing 500 a., 100 a. being conveyed. Susan, wife of John Richardson. Wit: Edward Cooke, Henry Turner. Acknowledged Dec 1 1674. Edward Sauvage, Clk.

3 Old 78/Jan 15 1673/Robert Harwood of Talbot County, Planter to Edmond Brannock of Dorchester County: "Harwood's Choice" on Fishing Creek and Little Choptank River, containing 150 a. more or less. Acknowledged Nov 3 1674 by Stephen Gary, Atty for Grantor. Edward Sauvage, Clk. Power of Atty witnessed by John Sumner, George Satterwight.

3 Old 79/Jul 18 1674/John Richardson of Dorchester County, Planter and Susanna his wife to Simon Richardson and John Yeale (Yale) of the same County, Planter: "Goodridge's Choice" on Cabin Creek adj land of Timothy Gutheridge and containing 300 a. more or less. Wit: Thomas Morris, William Chisam, Cornelius Haley. Acknowledged Aug 2 1674. Edward Sauvage, Clk. Assignment of the above land from Simon Richardson and John Yale to John Richardson, dated Mar 3 1674. Witnessed by John Rue, John Eavns.

3 Old 81/Nov 12 1674/John Richardson of Dorchester County, Planter to John Evans of Northumberland County, Virginia, planter: "Tract or helf tract" of land called "Goodridges Choice" on Cabin Creek adj land of Andrew Gray and containing 300 a. more or less. Susanna, wife of John Richardson. Wit:

Richard Girling, John Yale, Andrew Gray. Acknowledged Mar 4 1674 by John
Richardson andGeorge Prouse, Atty for Susanna Richardson. Edward Sauvage,
Clk. Power of Atty witnessed by George Watts, Stephen Dardan. Bond mentions
land as containing 150 a.

3 Old 83/Mar 1 1674/John Rawlings and Philadelphia his wife of Dorchester
County, Boatwright to John Edwards, planter: "St. Patrick" adj land laid out
for Henry Turner and containing 100 a. more or less. Wit: George Downs,
Michaell Basey. Acknowledged Mar 3 1674 by John Rawlings and Thomas Wall,
Atty for Philadelphia Rawlings.

3 Old 85/Jun 2 1675/John Richardson of Dorchester County Planter to William
Brice of the same place, Carpenter: One moyety of "Goodridges Choyce" on
Cabin treek adj land of Timothy Goodridge and containing 300 a., 150 a. being
conveyed. Susanna, wife of John Richardson. Wit: Bartholomew Ennalls,
Edward Sauvage. Acknowledged Jun 2 1675. Edward Sauvage, Clk.

3 Old 86/Jun 2 1675/John Rawlings, Boatwright and John Brookes, Chirurgeon,
of Dorchester County to John Reed of Northumberland Count, Virginia, "Taylor":
"Triangle," adj land of George Richardson and containing 100 a. more or less.
Wit: Gournay Crow, Anthony Dawson. Acknowledged Jun 2 1675. Edward Sauvage,
Clk. Power of Atty from John Reed to Henry Bradley of Dorchester County,
planter. Witnessed by Peter Pretly and Henry Howard. Thos Hobson, Notary
Public.

3 Old 88/May 25 1675/John Rawlings of Dorchester County, Boatwright to Robert
Winsmore of the same county, Chyrurgion: "Woodthorp" on Transquakin River
containing 200 a. more or less. Philadelphia Rawlings, wife of John Rawlings.
Wit: Arthur Wright, William Worgin, William Willoby. Acknowledged Jun 2 1675.
Edward Sauvage, Clk.

3 Old 90/Sep 1 1675/John Rawlings to Benjamin Hunt: "Masons Hoppyard" on
Transquakin River containing 150 a. Also "Strawberry Gerden" containing 150
a. Also "Whitelady Fields" now in the occupation of Richard Dawson on Transquakin River, containing 100 a. Also "Madens Choyce" containing 100 a. Also
a parcel of land at the head of Transquakin River containing 600 a. Also
"Dover" containing 1000 a. at the head of the North East Branch of Transquakin River called Chickanoquomicquo Branch. Wit: John Jones, William Lowe.
Acknowledged the last day :of September, 1675 before Robert Winsmore and Henry
Trippe. Edward Sauvage, Clk.

3 Old 91/Aug 7 1675/Stephen Beeson and John Gootier (Gautier) both of Dor-
chester County, Planters to William Ford of the same place, Gent.: "Carlyle"
on Blackwater, containing 100 a. more or less. Also "Browell Stone" on
Blackwater, containing 100 a. more or less. Also "Anchor and Hope" on Black-
water containing 200 a. more or less. Margrett, wife of John Gootier
(Gautier). Wit: A. Wright, William Willobey, Francis Oxman, Katherine
Cottle, William Dossey. Acknowledged Aug 7 1675 before Robert Winsmore and
Thomas Skinner, Justices. Edward Sauvage, Clk.

3 Old 94/Nov 2 1675/Peter Underwood of Dorchester County to John Wheatley,
Planter: 1/2 of "Castle Haven" containing 100 a. Wit: Edward Sauvage, John
Rawlings, A. Wright. Acknowledged Nov 2 1675. Edward Sauvage, Clk.

3 Old 95/Dec 15 1675/Stephen Beeson of Dorchester County, Planter to Francis
Taylor of the same place, Planter: Lease of "Breda" and "Jackett" on Blackwater. Wit: Ralph Wells, Robert Dix.

3 Old 96/Jan 4 1675/William Ford of Dorchester County, Gent., Rebecca Preston and Elizabeth Preston, relict of James Preston late of Calvert County, deceased to William Wroughton of Dorchester County, Planter: "Stone Wick" on Hungar River containing 150 a. more or less. Wit: Thomas Taylor, John Rawlings. Acknowledged Feb 1 1675. Edward Sauvage, Clk.

3 Old 97/Jan 3 1675/John Pitt of Talbot County, Merchant and Frances Pitt his wife to John Curtice of Dorchester County, Planter: "Hampton" on Hunting Creek, adj land laid out for Brett Dellander and containing 250 a. more or less. Wit: John Baynard, Humphrey Davis. Acknowledged Feb 1 1675 by George Robins, Atty for John Pitt and Frances Pitt. Edward Sauvage, Clk.

3 Old 98/Jul 10 1675/William Jones of Dorchester County, Planter to Raymond Stapleford of the same County, Gent.: "Keenes Rest" on Hungar River, containing 100 a. more or less. Wit: John Offley, Gournay Crowe. Acknowledged Feb 1 1675. Edward Sauvage, Clk.

3 Old 100/Jul 10 1674/William Jones of Dorchester County, Planter to Raymond Staplefort of the same County, Gent.: "All Three of Us," "in a river called Limbo Harbour in a creek of the said river called Russells Creeke," containing 100 a. more or less. Wit: John Offley, Gournay Crowe. Acknowledged Feb 1 1675. Edward Sauvage, Clk.

3 Old 101/Jan 26 1675/Stephen Sealous of Dorchester County, Planter to William Jones of the same place, Planter: "Sealous Chance" on Hungar River containing 50 a. Mary, wife of Stephen Sealous. Wit: Richard Tubman, Samuel Millington. Acknowledged Feb 1 1675 by Raymond Staplefort, Atty for Grantor. Edward Sauvage, Clk.

3 Old 103/Jan 26 1675/William Wroughton of Dorchester County to James Moadsley of the same place, Planter: "Staplefort Lott" and "Andrews Chance" on Hunger River; "Staplefort Lot" containing 100 a. and "Andrews Chance" containing 100 a. and "Andrews Chance" containing 6 a. Joanna, wife of William Wroughton. Wit: John Rawlins, William Robson, William Jones. Acknowledged Feb 1 1675. Edward Sauvage, Clk.

3 Old 105/Jan 4 1675/Thomas Taylor of Dorchester County, Gent. to Edward Sauvage, of the same place, Gent.: Moyety or 1/2 of a parcel of land called "Worgins Chance" purchased from Henry Turner, containing 25 a. Also a tract adj the afsd 25 a., containing 50 a. Wit: Henry Trippe, John Brooke. Acknowledged Feb 3 1675.

3 Old 106/Jan 4 1675/Thomas Scott of Dorchester County, Planter to Jeremy Markeham of the same place, Planter: "Scotts Hall" on Fishing Creek and Little Choptank River containing 50 a. more or less. Wit: John Dossey, William Dossey. Acknowledged Mar 7 1675. Edward Sauvage, Clk.

3 Old 107/Nov 3 1674/Thomas Wall of Dorchester County, Planter and Alse his wife to William Worgin and Alice his wife of the same county, Inholder: "Snake Poynt" containing 100 a. on Little Choptank River and Fishing Creek. Wit: Ri. Gorsuch., Ralph Wells, Gourney Crowe. Acknowledged Nov 3 1674. Edward Sauvage, Clk. Assigned by William Worgin to Thomas Wall Feb 18 1675. Assignment witnessed by A. Wright, Ann Mason.

3 Old 109/Feb 14 1672/Richard Gibbs of Percheham, Worcestershire, England, Merchant to William Brett of Dorchester County, Merchant: Part of "Armstrong's Folly" containing 200 a. more or less. Wit: Thomas Pattison, Edward Sauvage, A. Wright. Acknowledged Sep 2 1673 by Richard Gibbs to

Arthur Wright, Atty for William Brett. Edward Sauvage, Clk. Assignment of the above land from William Brett to Henry Mitchell of the Clifts, dated Dec 1 1673. Witnessed by John Malyus, Henry Heyd, Armigall Greenwood. Acknowledged Mar 7 1675. Edward Sauvage, Clk.

3 Old 111/Jul 30 1676/William Sharpe of Talbot County, Planter to John Pollard of Dorchester County, Gent.: "Marsh Land" on Little Choptank Bay and Back Creek containing 150 a. Also "Sharps Outlett" on Little Choptank River and Clatter Creek, adj land of Isaac Abram and containing 50 a. Also "Sharps Desire" on Little Choptank River and Clatter Creek adj land of Isaac Abram and containing 50 a. Wit: Gournay Crow, John Hungerford, Thomas Newman. Acknowledged Aug 2 1676 before Robert Winsmore, William Stephens, Henry Trippe, Stephen Gary and Charles Hutchins, Justices. Edward Sauvage, Clk.

3 Old 113/Sep 1 1675/Robert Collier of Dorchester County to Henry Mathews of "Northampton County in accomack": "Colliers Adventure" on Nanticoke River, containing 250 a. Wit: Bartholomew Ennalls, Charles Hutchins. Acknowledged Aug 2 1676 before William Stephens and Henry Trippe, Justices. Edward Sauvage, Clk.

3 Old 115/Sep 1 1675/Robert Collier of Dorchester County to John Hudson of "Northampton County in accomack": "Windsor" on the NW Branch of Nanticoke River, containing 350 a. Wit: Bartholomew Ennalls, Charles Hutchins. Acknowledged Aug 2 1676 before William Stephens and Henry Trippe, Justices. Edward Sauvage, Clk.

3 Old 116/Sep 1 1676/Daniel Clarke of Dorchester County, Gent. to "Mary Wood the daughter of Mary Wood now the wife of Anthony Taylor": "Charles Range" NW Branch of Transquakin River adj land of Thomas Taylor and Henry Turner and containing 200 a. Wit: Ed. Sauvage, Henry Turner. Acknowledged Sep 6 1676. Edward Sauvage, Clk.

3 Old 117/Apr 1 1676/John Hudson of Dorchester County, Planter to John Southey, Planter and John Button, Cooper: "Turkey Point" on Blackwater River containing 100 a. more or less. Wit: Gournay Crowe, Peter Stoaks, John Hungerford. Acknowledged Sep 6 1676 before Robert Winsmore and William Stephens, Justices. Edward Sauvage, Clk.

3 Old 118/Apr 8 1675/William Buttler of Talbot County, Planter to Simon Richardson of Dorchester County, Planter: Land on Cabin Creek adj land of Nicholas Homes and Containing 100 a., being part of "Goodridges Choyce" which contains 1000 a. in all. Wit: Henry Montague, William Brice. Acknowledged Sep 6 1676 by Arthur Wright, Atty for William Buttler. Edward Sauvage, Clk.

3 Old 120/Jun 2 1676/Robert Francis and Peter Baucomb, both of the Province of Delaware, to John Richardson of Dorchester County: "Hogg Poynt" on Hogg Creek, containing 300 a. more or less. Wit: Francis Whittwell, Edmond Ryall, William Wattson, William Chesum, Thomas Alexander. Acknowledged Sep 6 1676 by William Worgin, Atty for Grantors. Edward Sauvage, Clk. Power of Atty shows land divided 200 a. to Robert Francis and 100 a. to Peter Baucomb.

3 Old 122/Jun 1 1674/Arthur Wright of Dorchester County, Planter to James Browne of said County: "Five Pines" on Castle Haven Bay containing 106 a. more or less. Abigaill, wife of Arthur Wright. Wit: Edward Sauvage, Thomas Gilbert. Acknowledged Jan 2 1674 before Robert Winsmore and Bartholomew Ennalls, Justices. Edward Sauvage, Clk. Assignment from James Brown to Arthur Wright Nov 7 1676. Witnessed by William Stephens, Henry Trippe. Acknowledged in open Court Nov 8 1676. Edward Sauvage, Clk.

3 Old 124/Feb 15 1674/John Avery of Dorchester County, Shipwright, to Anne
Daldson: In consideration of their approaching marriage, he conveys all his
property, especially his home on Oyster Creek, to her for her lifetime after
his decease and at her death to their children; if they have no issue, the
property to go to grantor's son, John Avery, of London, England. Wit: Thomas
Pattison, Ann Pattison. Proved in open Court Nov 8 1676 by Thomas Pattison to
be the act and deed of John Avery to Ann his wife. Edward Sauvage, Clk.

3 Old 124/Jan 2 1676/John Edmondson of Talbot County, Gent. and Sarah his
wife to James Noell of Dorchester County: "Oyster Point" adj land of Anthony
LeCompte and containing 50 acres more or less. Wit: Thomas Gilbert, John
Standley. Acknowledged Jan 2 1676. Edward Sauvage, Clk.

3 Old 125/Feb 4 1676/Cuthbert Phelphs (Phelps) of Talbot County, Planter to
John Richardson of Dorchester County, Planter: "Wakefield" on Hunting Creek
containing 300 a. more or less. Also "Huntington" on the said creek adj land
laid out for Thomas Langden and containing 400 a. Frances, wife of Cuthbert
Phelps. Wit: Thomas Williams, William Jones, Edward Cooke. Acknowledged
Feb 6 1676 in open Court to John Brooke, Atty for John Richardson. Edward
Sauvage, Clk.

3 Old 127/Jan 6 1676/John Rawlings of Dorchester County, Boatwright to
William Willoby, "Plaisterer" and Jafad Griffin, Planter: "Maydens Choice" on
Transquakin River adj "Exchance" and containing 100 a. Also "White Lady
Fields" adj "Maidens Choyce" and containing 100 a. Philadelphia, wife of
John Rawlings. Wit: Henry Turner, Anthony Dawson. Acknowledged Feb 6 1676
in open Court. Edward Sauvage, Clk. Margrett Rawlings, daughter of John
Rawlings.

3 Old 129/Feb 4 1676/John Rawlings, Boatwright of Dorchester County to John
Brooke, Chyrurgeon of the same County: "two parcells of land containing five
hundred a. the first moyety containing three hundred a. called by the name of
Rawlings Folly lying on the North side of Transquaking River ... also the
other moyety containing two hundred acres called the Raing adjoyning to the
afd. three hundred acres." Wit: William Stephens, Edward Sauvage. Acknowledged in open court Feb 6 1676. Edward Sauvage, Clk.

3 Old 130/Mar 5 1676/William Ford of Dorchester County, Gent. to William
Merchant of the same place, planter: Land on Blackwater Creek containing 550
a. more or less, called "Hereford." Wit: William Stephens, John Edwards.
Acknowledged in open Court Mar 7 1676. Edward Sauvage, Clk. Alienation money
paid John Hungerford, Sub Sherr. to Thomas Taylor, Feb 19 1678/9. Addition
to deed, dated Mar 6 1676, describes land as including all of a neck called
Jones Neck and "land lying on the back of the Land now in the tenour and
occupation of John Southee."

3 Old 132/Mar 1 1676/William Ford of Dorchester County, Gent. to Thomas
Flowers of the same place planter: "Haverdegrace" in the fork of Blackwater
River, containing 100 a. more or less. Wit: William Stephens, John Edwards.
Acknowledged in open Court Mar 7 1676. Edward Sauvage, Clk.

3 Old 133/Mar 1 1676/William Ford of Dorchester County, Gent. to his kins-
woman Elizabeth the wife of Robert Dicks of the same place planter: "Anchor
and Hope" on the west side of the Northern Branch of Blackwater River, containing 200 a. Wit: William Stephens, John Edwards. Acknowledged Mar 7 1676.
Edward Sauvage, Clk.

3 Old 134/Mar 6 1676/John Rawlings and Philadelphia his wife to John Salisbury of Dorchester County, Carpenter: Land called "The Prosperity" (?) on

Transquakin River adj "Rawlings Folly" and containing 300 a. Wit: Thomas Gilbert, Andrew Gray. Acknowledged in open Court Mar 17 1676. Edward Sauvage, Clk.

3 Old 135/Mar 25 1677/William Ford of Dorchester County to Howell Powell of Talbot County: "East Town" on the East side of Blackwater River, near the head of Cabin Branch, containing 80 a. Wit: Edward Cooke, John Haslwood. Acknowledged Mar 25 1677 before Henry Trippe and John Brooke.

3 Old 135/Dec 10 1676/Henry Mathews of Northampton County, Virginia to Mathew Patrick, planter of the county afsd: "Colliers Adventure" on Nanticoke River containing 250 a. more or less, formerly granted to Robert Collier Sep 7 1674 and assigned by him to Henry Mathews Sep 1 1675. Wit: William Foster, John Hudson. Acknowledged Jun 5 1677. John Lyon, atty for Henry Mathews; Charles Hutchins, atty for Mathew Patrick.

3 Old 137/Jan 6 1676/John Rawlings, Boatwright to William Willowbey, "Plaisterer" and Japhat Griffin, Planter: "Maidens Choyce" adj "The Exchange" and containing 100 a. more or less. Also "White Lady Fields" adj "Maidens Choyce" and containing 100 a. Philadelphia, wife of John Rawlings. Wit: Henry Turner, Anthony Dawson. Acknowledged Feb 6 1676. Edward Sauvage, Clk. Interest of William Willobey in the above land assigned to Japhat Griffin, Jun 6 1677. Assignment witnessed by John Brooke and Anthony Hardacre.

3 Old 138/Aug 1677/Richard Meekins of Dorchester County, Planter to Timothy MacNamara of Somerset County, Planter: "Apes Hill" at the mouth of Hungar River containing 50 a. more or less. Joanna, wife of Richard Meekins. Wit: John Brooke, William Stephens. Acknowledged Aug 17 1677. Bond witnessed by John Brooke, Thomas Gilbert.

3 Old 140/Jun 5 1677/Thomas Taylor of Dorchester County, Gent. to Humphrey Hubbart of the same County: "Taylors Hap" at the head of Hudsons Creek, containing 50 a. more or less. Wit: William Dossey, John Hudson. Acknowledged Aug 7 1677. Edward Sauvage, Clk.

3 Old 141/Jul 31 1677/John Rawlings of Dorchester County to William Stephens of the same County, Gent.: "Exchange" on the Western Branch of Transquakin River adj land of Ishmaell Wright and containing 150 a. more or less. Philadelphia, wife of John Rawlings. Wit: Thomas Bowman, Humphrey Hubbert. Acknowledged Aug 7 1677. Edward Sauvage, Clk.

3 Old 143/May 8 1676/Patent from Charles, Lord Baltimore to John Richardson of Talbot County: "North hampton" at the mouth of Hunting Creek adj lands of Thomas Dougley and William Eldridge and containing 100 a. more or less. Assignment from John Richardson to William Wattson and William Cheesum, dated ... 21 1676. Witnessed by Edward Cooke, George Prouse. Acknowledged Nov 6 1677. Edward Sauvage, Clk.

3 Old 144/Nov 9 1678/Ann Coppen of Dorchester County, Widow to Charles Hutchins of the same County, Gent.: "Weston" on Nanticoke River, granted by patent to Gerome White, Esquire and conveyed to Ann Coppen by Thomas Taylor of the Ridge of Annarundell County, atty for George White of Runwell in the County of Essex, brother and heir of said Gerome White; adj land laid out for Timothy Goodridge and containing 1000 a. more or less. Wit: Lewis Jones, Thomas Hicks, Robert Olliver. Acknowledged Dec 3 1678 by Thomas Daniell, Atty for Ann Coppen, before William Stephens and Henry Bradley.

3 Old 146/Nov 22 1678/Benjamin Granger of Dorchester County, planter to John Pollard of the same County, Gent.: Land on Little Choptank River called Devideing Point" containing 100 a. more or less. Mary, wife of Benjamin

Granger. Wit: Gload (Claude, Cload) Lewis, William Evans, Peter Parry, Thomas Pattison. Acknowledged Dec 2 1678. Phineas Blankwood, Atty for Benjamin Granger. Wm Smithson, Clk.

3 Old 148/Nov 20 1678/John Reed of Northumberland County, Virginia to Jonathan Bateman of the same County, planter: Land on Transquakin River containing 100 a. more or less, sold to said John Reed by John Rawlings and John Brookes and adj land of George Richardson. Wit: Thomas Daniell, Edward Fisher. Acknowledged Dec 3 1678 by Lewis Jones, Atty for John Reed, before William Stephens and Bartholomew Ennalls. William Smithson, Clk. Charles Hutchins, Atty for Jonathan Bateman.

3 Old 150/Dec 2 1678/Phineas Blankwood of Dorchester County, Schoolmaster to John Pollard of the same County, Gent.: "Blood Point" on Little Choptank River at the mouth of Slaughter Creek, containing 100 a. more or less. Acknowledged Dec 2 1678 before William Stephens, Stephen Garry. William Smithson, Clk.

3 Old 151/Jun 5 1678/Patrick Mullekin of Talbot County, planter to John Pollard of Dorchester County, Gent.: "Mullekin's Land" in the bay behind St. James Point and on St. Stephen's Creek, containing 400 a. more or less. Wit; John Brooke, Humphrey Hubbert, Phineas Blackwood. Acknowledged Jun 5 1678. William Smithson, Clk.

3 Old 153/Sep 13 1678/Daniell Clarke of Dorchester County, heir and Executor of Edward Sauvage, deceased, to William Tregoe the Elder of Bristol, Mariner: "Worgin's Adventure" on Little Choptank River and Fishing Creek, adj land of Robert Harwood and containing 50 a. more or less. Wit: James Moadsley, John Phillips. Acknowledged Sep 14 1678 before William Stephens and Stephen Garry. William Smithson, Clk.

3 Old 154/Sep 13 1678/Daniell Clarke of Little Choptank in Dorchester County, Gent., heir and Executor of Edward Sauvage deceased to William Tregoe the Elder of Bristol, Mariner: 1/2 of Land purchased by Edward Sauvage from Thomas Taylor, called "Worgan's Chance," containing 25 a.; also 50 a. adj afsd 25 a., 75 a. in all. Wit: James Moadsley, John Phillips. Acknowledged Sep 14 1678 before William Stephens and Stephen Gary. William Smithson, Clk.

3 Old 155/Sep 13 1678/Daniell Clarke of Little Choptank in Dorchester County, heir and Executor of Edward Sauvage, deceased to William Tregoe the Elder of Bristol, Mariner: Part of "Worgins Chance" containing 50 a. of land, 25 a. being conveyed. Wit: James Moadsley, John Phillips. Acknowledged Sep 14 1678 before William Stephens and Stephen Garry. William Smithson, Clk.

3 Old 156/Apr 1 1679/Timothy McNamara of Dorchester County, Planter to John Pritchett of the same County, planter: "Apes Hill" at the mouth of Hungar River, containing 50 a. more or less. Wit: John Phillips, Thomas Pattison. Acknowledged Apr 1 1679. William Smithson, Clk.

3 Old 158/Apr 1 1679/John Pritchett of Dorchester County, planter to John Prout of the same County, planter: 16 a., a small neck on the lowermost part of "Apes Hill." Wit: John Phillips, Thomas Pattison. Acknowledged Apr 1 1679. William Smithson, Clk.

3 Old 159/Jan 8 1678/Lewis Griffin of Dorchester County to Timothy McNamara of the same County, Planter: 50 a. near the mouth of Transquakin, patented to Henry Hooper. Wit: Thomas Pattison, John Kembell, John Pritchett. Acknowledged Jan 8 1678. William Smithson, Clk.

3 Old 161/Sep 2 1679/John Richardson of Dorchester County, planter to Thomas Flowers of the same County, planter: "Marsh Point" on Hogg Creek, containing

300 a. more or less. Wit: Henry Howard, Richard Owen, William Dorsey. Susanna, wife of John Richardson. Acknowledged Sep 2 1679. William Smithson, Clk.

3 Old 162/Aug 1 1679/Rebecca Preston of Dorchester County, Spinster to Sarah (Preston) Ford, widow of the same County: "Widow's Lot," being 1/2 of a tract called "Horne" on Virgins Creek, adj land of John Jenkins and containing 600 a. more or less, devised by Richard Preston late of Calvert County, deceased in his Last Will and Testament to his daughters Rebecca and Sarah. Wit: William Smithson, Edward Pinder, Thomas Jones. Acknowledged Aug 17 1679 before William Stephens and John Brooke. William Smithson, Clk.

3 Old 164/Aug 1 1679/Sarah (Preston) Ford of Dorchester County, widow to Rebecca Preston, of the same County, spinster: "Maidens Lot" being 1/2 of a tract called "Horne" on Virgins Creek adj land of John Jenkins and containing 600 a. more or less, devised by Richard Preston late of Calvert County deceased in his Last Will and Testament to Rebecca and Sarah. Wit: William Smithson, Edward Pinder, Thomas Jones. Acknowledged Aug 17 1679 before William Stephens and John Brooke. William Smithson, Clk.

3 Old 166/Jan 8 1678/Andrew Insley of Dorchester County, planter to John Gooty of the same County, planter: Land on Transquakin River containing 50 a. more or less, called "Insley's Point." Wit: Thomas Pattison, Timothy McNamara, John Pritchett, Lewis Griffin. Acknowledged Jan 8 1678. William Smithson, Clk.

3 Old 167/Apr 1 1679/Thomas Snell of Dorchester County, Merchant to Richard Cornish of Talbot County, Merchant: 150 a. lately purchased from Thomas Taylor of Dorchester County, planter, being 1/2 of a tract of 300 a. on Cabin Creek purchased by said Thomas Taylor from Andrew Gray. Wit: William Combs, John Walls, William Cross. Acknowledged in open Court Apr 1 1679. William Smithson, Clk.

3 Old 168/1677/Samuel Jackson of Somerset County, planter, George Watts of Talbot County, planter and Anne Watts his wife to John Curtis of Dorchester County: "Rochester" on Watts Creek on the NE Branch of Great Choptank River, containing 100 a. more or less. Also "Indian Quarter" adj "Rochester" and containing 100 a. more or less. Wit: Charles Hutchins, George Watts Jr, George Cowley, Samuel Hatton.

3 Old 169/Reference to patent of "Dales Right" on Little Choptank River, Hudson's Creek and Dales Cove, granted May 10 1671 to William Stephens.

3 Old 169/Sep 2 1678/William Brice of Dorchester County, planter to Edward Pinder of the same County: "Buttwells Choice" near the head of Little Choptank River adj land of Robert Winsmore and containing 100 a. more or less. Wit: John Brooke, Benjamin Hunt. Acknowledged Sep 3 1678 before HenryTrippe and John Brooke. William Smithson, Clk.

3 Old 170/Aug 7 1679/Jeremiah Markham of Dorchester County to James Harper of the same County: "Scotts Hall" and "Markhams Desire," each tract containing 50 a. more or less, on Fishing Creek and little Choptank River. Wit: H. Hubbard, Ezekiel Fogg. Acknowledged Aug 1679. William Smithson, Cik.

3 Old 172/Aug 18 1679/Phillip Shapleigh of Northumberland County, Virginia to William Travers of Dorchester County: "Shapleighs Chance" on Hoopers Island, on Tar Bay and Fishing Creek, adj William Chaplaine's land and containing 117 a. more or less; also land in Hungar River and Fishing Creek containing 50 a. more or less. Wit: William Hill, John Phillips, John Rowland. Deliver-

ed Sep 12 1679 by John Phillips in behalf of Philip Shapleigh, before Bartholomew Ennalls and John Alford. William Smithson, Clk.

3 Old 173/Aug 7 1679/Thomas Pattison of Dorchester County, Wine cooper to Joseph Serjant of Dorchester County: "Canterbury" at the head of Transquakin River, adj "Linkwoods" and containing 225 a. more or less. Wit: H. Hubbard, John Lawrence, John Ross. Ann, wife of Thomas Pattison. Acknowledged in open Court Aug 7 1679. William Smithson, Clk.

3 Old 175/Aug 18 1679/Power of Atty from Philip Shapleigh to John Phillips re land on Hoopers Island sold by Shapleigh to William Travis of "Pattuxon." Proved Sep 12 1679 before Bartholomew Ennalls and John Alford. William Smithson, Clk.

3 Old 175/Nov 6 1679/Sarah Newton, wdow of Thomas Newton, to her daughter Elizabeth Newton and her heirs, or if she leaves no issue, to John Newton and Thomas Newton, Sons of Sarah Newton: "Humphreys Fortune" devised to said Sarah Newton by Samuel Pritchett in his Last Will and Testament, containing 250 a. more or less. Date of death of Samuel Pritchett Jan 26 1678. Personalty devised to Elizabeth Newton or, if she dies before becoming of age, to Sarah Tregoe the wife of William Tregoe the younger of the City of Bristol, Mariner. Wit: Henry Howard, Edward Pinder. Acknowledged Nov 6 1679 before Thomas Taylor and John Alford. William Smithson, Clk.

3 Old 177/Aug 7 1679/John Richardson of Dorchester County, planter to John Alford of Dorchester County, Gent.: Five parcels of land containing 1300 a. more or less in all. "Fox Hill" adj land of George Richardson, adj Marshy Creek and containing 200 a.; "Wakefield" on Hunting Creek containing 300 a.; "Skipton" at the head of Fox Creek, adj land of Daniel Jones and John Edmondson and containing 200 a.; "Eldridge" adj land laid out for Hopkins Davis and containing 200 a.; "Huntington" on Hunting Creek adj land laid out for Thomas Langden and containing 400 a. more or less. Wit: Thomas Taylor, H. Hubbard, Richard Owen. Susanna, wife of John Richardson. Acknowledged Aug 8 1679. William Smithson, Clk.

3 Old 179/Oct 29 1677/William Willoughby of Dorchester County, Planter to Marke Mitchell of the same County, Planter: "Raxall" adj land of Anthony Lecompte, Gent., late decd. and containing 50 a. Hannah, wife of William Willoughby. Wit: Benj. Hunt, Japhat Griffin. Acknowledged Sep 4 1679. William Smithson, Clk.

3 Old 180/Aug 6 1678/William Stephens of Little Choptank River, Gent, to William Keyson of Little Choptank River: "Dales Right" on Little Choptank River, Hudsons Creek and Dales Cove, containing 100 a. more or less. Acknowledged Aug 6 William Smithson, Clk.

3 Old 181/Sep 4 1678/John Brooke of Dorchester County Gent to Humphrey Hubbert of the same County: "Indian Quarter" containing 50 a.; and "Brookes Outhold" adj the afsd 50 a. and containing 100 a. Wit: Phineas Blackwood, Thomas Seamans. Acknowledged Sep 4 1678. William Smithson, Clk.

3 Old 182/Nov 7 1678/John Salisbury of Dorchester County, Planter to John Brooke, Chyrurgion of the same County: 40 a. of a tract of 300 a. on the NW branch of Transquakin River, between Mullikins Land and the land of John Rawlings formerly Michall Mason. Wit: Anthony Dallany, James Fielding. Acknowledged Nov 7 1678. William Smithson, Clk.

3 Old 183/Aug 4 1678/Anthony Dawson, Carpenter of Dorchester County, and Rebecca his wife to John Brooke of Dorchester County Chyrurgion: 300 a.

called "Dawson's Chance" adj "Malden" on Armstrong's Bay and adj "Ceader Point." Wit: George Cowley, John Coughlan. Acknowledged Aug 4 1678. William Smithson, Clk.

3 Old 185/Aug 30 1677/Robert Taylor of Dorchester County, Planter to Rice Vaughan of the same County, Planter: "Taylors Purchase" on Transquakin River, containing 100 a. more or less. Wit: Lawrance Woodnett, John Forster. Acknowledged Jun 4 1678. William Smithson, Clk.

3 Old 186/May 1679/Henry Mitchell of the Clifts in Calvert County, Planter to Jeffery Meanely of the Clifts in Calvert County, Planter: "Ceader Point" containing 150 a. more or less, formerly sold by Mitchell to William Stephens. Wit: George Parker, James Crawford. Acknowledged Dec 2 1679 before John Taylor and John Alford, Justices. William Smithson, Clk. Depositions of Benj. Hunt and Edward Pinder re bounds of the land of William Stephens.

3 Old 189/Dec 18 1679/Release from Ezekiel Fogg to Elizabeth Brown, widow of Thomas Brown deceased. Wit: Edward Cooke, William Smithson, Henry Howard

3 Old 189/Apr 1 1679/John Brooke of Dorchester County, Gent. and Katherine his wife to Thomas Taylor of the same County, Gent.: "Trippes Ridge" on Little Choptank River at the head of Trippes Creek, adj land formerly laid out for Michall Brooks and containing 150 a. more or less. Wit: William Smithson, John Hillins, Henry Turner. Acknowledged Apr 1 1679. William Smithson, Clk.

3 Old 190/Apr 1 1679/John Brooke of Dorchester County, Gent. and Katherine his wife to Thomas Taylor of the same County, Gent.: Land between Jordan's Point and Mannings Point, adj land of Thomas Jordan containing 250 a. more or less. Wit: William Smithson, John Hollins, Henry Turner. Acknowledged in open Court Apr 1 1679. William Smithson, Clk.

3 Old 192/Nov 4 1679/William Merchant of Dorchester County and Rachell his wife to James Agg of the same County: Assignment of lands previously assigned to Merchant by Thomas Pratt of Ann Arundell County. Wit: John Brooke, Henry Howard, John Salisbury. Acknowledged Nov 4 1679. William Smithson, Clk.

3 Old 193/Nov 4 1679/Richard Meekins and Joanna his wife of Dorchester County, planter to George Hooper of the same County, Cooper: "Plain Dealing" on Hungar River and Charles Creek, containing 50 a. more or less. Wit: Phineas Blackwood, William Shinton. Acknowledged Nov 4 1679. William Smithson, Clk. Bond witnessed by Thos Seamans, John Hungerford.

3 Old 194/Mar 28 1678/Richard Meekins of Dorchester County to Joseph Stanway of the same County: "Southampton" on Hungar River and Fox Creek containing 100 a. more or less. Wit: Thomas Hartly, Robert Norman. Acknowledged Nov 4 1679. William Smithson, Clk.

3 Old 195/Jan 6 1679/John Edmondson of Tread haven in Talbot County to Bartholomew Ennalls of Dorchester County: 500 a. more or less on Transquakin River. Wit: Thomas Taylor, Thomas Gilbert. Acknowledged Jan 6 1679. William Smithson, Clk.

3 Old 196/Aug 25 1677/Thomas Wall of Dorchester County, planter to John Forster of the same County, planter: Land on Little Choptank River and Fishing Creek called "Snake Point," containing 100 a. more or less. Wit: John Edwards, Morgan Jones, Anthony Taylor. Deed signed by Thomas Wall and Ales Wall. Acknowledged Nov 12 1677 before Bartholomew Ennalls and Henry Bradley. William Smithson, Clk.

3 Old 198/Apr 4 1679/John Rawlings, Inholder to James Peterkin, Mariner: Bond re Indentures of Lease dated Sep 16 1674 from John Rawlings and Phila-

delphia his wife to James Peterkin for "Plain Dealing" containing 200 a. more
or less. Wit: John Hollins, John Pope. Acknowledged Apr 1 1679. William
Smithson, Clk.

3 Old 198/Jan 12 167/Agreement re division of "Leverton" on Fishing Creek and
Little Choptank River containing 250 a. more or less, one Moyety having been
sold to William Ticke and the other moyety having been sold to Obadiah
Jenkins by Pater Sharpe of Calvert County, late deceased and afterwards sold
to Miles Mason late of this County deceased. William Teck for himself and
Peter Stoaks for the heirs of Miles Mason agree to a division of the land
made this day by Thomas Pattison, Deputy Surveyor for Dorchester County in
the presence of William Dossey and John Watterly. Acknowledged Mar 3 1679
before John Brooke and William Dorrington. William Smithson, Clk.

3 Old 198/May 4 1672/William Dorrington to Thomas Fisher: Lease of land on
the West side of Little Creek, divided by Little Creek from a tract sold by
said Dorrington to said Fisher on the East side of the Creek. Wit: Peter
Underwood, William Brice. Proved Mar 3 1679 by William Brice, one of the
Witnesses.

3 Old 199/Feb 20 1679/John Alford of Dorchester County, Gent. and Elizabeth
his wife to Jacob Loockerman of the same County, Gent.: "Musketer Quarter" on
Tobacco Stick Creek and Little Choptank River, containing 200 a. more or less.
Wit: Thomas Pattison, Henry Howard. Acknowledged Mar 3 1679/80. William
Smithson, Clk. Assignment from Stephen Gary of Dorchester County, Gent. to
Jacob Loockerman, of Gary's interest or claim to the afsd land. Clare, wife
of Stephen Gary.

3 Old 201/Jan 28 1679/John Tench of the City of Bristol, Mariner to Thomas
Taylor of Dorchester County, Gent.: "Tenches Hope" on Tripps Creek. Wit:
Stephen Garey, Thos Cooke, Rich. Pecocke. Acknowledged Mar 3 1679/80 by
William Smithson, Atty for John Tench. Power of Atty from John Tench of the
Kingdom of England, Mariner to William Smithson or Henry Howard to acknow-
ledge 200 a. called "Tenches Hope" to Majr. Thomas Taylor.

3 Old 202/Mar 1679/Sara Ford, widow of William Ford late of Dorchester County,
deceased to Edward Pinder of the same county, planter: In consideration that
the said Edward will provide for said Sara Ford and her three children
Samuell, Josias and Rebecca for seven years from the date of these presents
and will teach her three children to read and write, she "hath demised
granted sett and to farm lett unto him the said Edward Pinder" the "Widdow's
Lott" being one moyety of a tract called "Horne" on Virgins Creek adj
"Maidens Lott."

3 Old 203/May 30 1668/Daniel Clarke, planter to John Rawlings, Carpenter:
"Clarke's Neck" on Little Choptank and Clarkes Creek containing 250 a., adj
500 a. of Richard Preston's land. Wit: John Blane, Morris Matthie. Obliga-
tion of John Rawlings to convey the above land to Thomas Vaughan, dated Dec
18 1669, witnessed by John Wattkins and Thomas Tasker. Assignment from
Thomas Vaughan to Thomas Simmons of St. Mary's County for the above land,
dated Sep 13 1670, witnessed by Joseph Brough and Joseph Woodard. Acknowledged Sep 5 1671 by Arthur Wright, Atty for John Rawlings, to Thomas
Simmons. Edward Sauvage, Clk. Assignment from John Rawlings to Thomas
Simmons witnessed by Wm Worgin and John Wakefield. Power of Atty from John
Rawlings to Arthur Wright witnessed by Wm Worgin and Henry Beckwith.

3 Old 205/Oct 5 1671/William Dorrington of Dorchester County to Thomas
Fisher, planter of the same County: Part of 500 a. called "Busby" on Great

Choptank River and Little Creek. 100 a. conveyed. Wit: John Rawlings, John Clements. Acknowledged Sep 5 1671. Edward Sauvage, Clk.

3 Old 205/Mar 6 1670/Timothy Goodridge, planter of Talbot County to Edward Roe: 200 a. on Cabin Creek, part of 1000 a. called "Goodridge's Choyce." Wit: William Battle, John Wright. Acknowledged Mar 7 1670. Edward Sauvage, Clk. Assignment from Edward Roe and Mary his wife to Nicholas Holmes, witnessed by John Clements and William Prisk. Acknowledged Sep 5 1671 by John Clements, Atty for Edward Roe and Mary his wife, to Nicholas Holmes. Edward Sauvage, Clk.

3 Old 207/Sep 21 1663/Andrew Skinner of Talbot County to Thomas Martine: "Castle Haven" containing 100 a. more or less. Wit: William Fowler, Richd. Girling. Assignment from Thomas Martine of Talbot County to Peter Underwood of Dorchester County, dated Nov 7 1671, witnessed by John Brook and Henry Tripp. Acknowledged Nov 7 1671. Edward Sauvage, Clk.

3 Old 207/Nov 3 1671/Daniel Jones of Talbot County, planter to John Kirk of the same County: Part of 300 a. which formerly belonged to Richard Hughs; 200 a. more or less on Hughs Creek conveyed. Mary, wife of Daniel Jones. Wit: Theophilus Incheverall, John Humberstone. Acknowledged Nov 7 1671. Edward Sauvage, Clk.

3 Old 208/Nov 7 1670/James Selby of Dorchester County, Gent. to Stephen Beeson and John Goteer of the same County: "Brambleston" on Blackwater containing 100 a. more or less. Signed by William Worgan, Administrator of James Selby. Wit: A. Wright, Tym. McNamara, Anthony Dawson. Acknowledged Nov 7 1671. Edward Sauvage, Clk.

3 Old 209/Nov 7 1671/James Selby of Dorchester County, Gent. to Stephen Beeson and John Gootier, Planters: "Anchor and Hope" on Blackwater containing 200 a. more or less. Signed by William Worgan, Admr. of James Selby. Wit: A. Wright, Timo. Macknamara, Anthony Dawson. Acknowledged Nov 7 1671. Edward Sauvage, Clk.

3 Old 210/Nov 7 1670/James Selby to Stephen Beeson and John Gootier:"Carlile" on Blackwater containing 100 a. more or less. Signed by William Worgan, Admr. of James Selby. Wit: A. Wright, Timo. Macknamara, Anthony Dawson. Acknowledged Nov 7 1671. Edward Sauvage, Clk.

3 Old 212/Nov 6 1671/Thomas Hooton Dorchester County, Planter to Thomas Broxome of the same County: 50 a. called "Hooton's Folly" on "an island called Hoopers Island and Chaplines Island," on Hungar River. Mary, wife of Thomas Hooton. Wit: Peter Blackwood, Rd. Rainer. Acknowledged Nov 7 1671. Edward Sauvage, Clk.

3 Old 213/Nov 1 1671/John Edmondson of Talbot to Nicholas Hackett of the same County: "Adventure" on Hunting Creek on the South side of Choptank River, adj lands of Cuthbert Phelpes and land of John Edmondson called "Skipton," and containing 300 a. more or less. Wit: Edward Wirckles, Robert Williams. Acknowledged Nov 7 1671. Edward Sauvage, Clk.

3 Old 213/Oct 9 1671/John Edmondson to John Holt and Andrew Purdo: "Bretts Hope" containing 600 a., formerly laid out for Brett Dalender on Smiths Creek. Wit: Anto. Mayle, Wm Kirom. Acknowledged Nov 7 1671 by John Edmondson, Atty for Brett Dallender. Edward Sauvage, Clk. Power of Atty from Brett witnessed by Andrew Bell and James Williams, Aug 20 1665.

3 Old 213/Nov 7 1671/Stephen Beeson and John Gootie to Arthur Wright and Henry Beckwith: "Stewarts Place" containing 300 a. on Little Choptank. Margaret, wife of John Gootie. Wit: Saml. Abbott, Timo. Macnamara, James Butler, Thos Gilbert. Acknowledged Nov 7 1671. Edward Sauvage, Clk.

3 Old 217/Nov 7 1671/Arthur Wright to Thomas Taylor: "Taylors Inheritance" on an Island on Slaughter Creek and St. John's Creek, containing 200 a. more or less. Abigail, wife of Arthur Wright. Acknowledged Nov 7 1671. Edward Sauvage, Clk.

3 Old 218/Nov 7 1671/Thomas Hooton, planter to Richard Butwell: "Hootons Choyce" on Blackwater, containing 100 a. more or less. Mary, wife of Thomas Hooton. Acknowledged Nov 7 1671. Edward Sauvage, Clk.

3 Old 219/Dec 1671/Stephen Garey of Little Choptank to Phineas Blackwood, Schoolmaster: 100 a. on the Bay behind St. James Creek, on Little Choptank River and Slaughter Creek, patented to said Stephen Garey Sep 1 1671. Acknowledged Dec 5 1671. Edward Sauvage, Clk.

3 Old 220/Oct 28 1671/John Garey of Calvert County, planter to John Mackeel of Dorchester County, planter: 150 a. called "Garey's Chance" on Little Choptank River and Fishing Creek patented to Garey Jul 29 1664; also 100 a. called "Timber Poynt," adj "Garey's Chance." Alice, wife of John Garey. Acknowledged Nov 7 1671. Edward Sauvage, Clk. Receipt of Thos Taylor, Sheriff, for alienation of above land, dated Nov 19 1671.

3 Old 222/Dec 4 1671/William Worgan, Executor of James Selby to Edmond Brannock, planter: "Appleby" laid out for Selby on Little Choptank River and Fishing Creek adj land formerly laid out for John Gather called "Gatherby," and containing 50 a. Wit: Thos. Vickars, Thomas Skinner, Edward Sauvage. Possession delivered in the presence of Stephen Garey and John Miles, Dec 7 1671. Acknowledged in Court Dec 5 1671. Edward Sauvage, Clk.

3 Old 224/Dec 5 1671/Thomas Newton of Dorchester County, planter to Francis Twyford of the same County, planter: "Georges Choyce" on Salt Marsh Creek and Little Choptank River, containing 100 a. more or less. Sarah, wife of Thomas Newton. Wit: A. Wright, Thos Ashley. Acknowledged Dec 5 1671. Edward Sauvage, Clk.

3 Old 225/May 15 1671/Andrew Insley of Dorchester County, planter to William Wroughton of the same County, planter: "Andrews Poynt" otherwise known as "Andrew's Chance" on Hungar River adj land formerly owned by John Lugers and containing 6 a. more or less, patented to sd. Insley Aug 20 1668. Wit: A. Wright, Lewis Griffith. Acknowledged Nov 7 1671. Edward Sauvage, Clk.

3 Old 227/Oct 16 1671/Raymond Staplefort of Dorchester County to Daniell Holland of the same County: "Commencement" patented to Staplefort Jul 3 1667, on Slaughter Creek and St. John's Creek and containing 100 a. more or less. Wit: John Phillips, William Jones, James Cross. Acknowledged Nov 7 1671. Edward Sauvage, Clk.

3 Old 229/Oct 16 1671/Raymond Staplefort of Dorchester County to Daniell Holland of the same County: 100 a. called "Commencement" patented to Staplefort Jul 17 1667 on St. Johns Creek, on an island. Wit: John Phillips, William Jones, James Crosse. Acknowledged Nov 7 1671. Edward Sauvage, Clk. Bond of Raymond Staplefort re 200 a. called "Commencement" sold to Daniell Holland, witnessed by John Phillips, William Jones and James Crosse and acknowledged Nov 7 1671.

3 Old 231/Jul 21 1671/Thomas Hooton (Hutton) of Dorchester County, planter to
James Modsley of the same County, planter: "Colliers Forrest" patented to
Hooton Aug 11 1668 on the east side of Hungar River containing 50 a. more or
less. Wit: William Johnes (Joanes), Richd. Cudman. Acknowledged Nov 7 1671.
Edward Sauvage, Clk.

3 Old 234/Nov 7 1671/Thomas Hooton of Dorchester County, planter to Godfrey
Cham of the same County, planter: "Black Walnut Point" on Transquakin River,
containing 50 a. more or less. Mary, wife of Thomas Hooton. Wit: John
Pollard, Phine. Blackwood. Acknowledged Nov 7 1671. Edward Sauvage, Clk.

3 Old 235/Dec 5 1671/John Edmondson of Talbot County, Mcht. to William
Willowby of Dorchester County, Plasterer: "Discovery" on Johns Creek adj
lands of Anthony LeCompte and John Stevens and containing 50 a. more or less.
Sarah, wife of John Edmondson. Wit: Thomas Ashley, Richard Owen. Acknowledged Dec 5 1671. Edward Sauvage, Clk.

3 Old 236/Jan 1 1671/William Willowby of Dorchester County, plasterer, to
Anthony LeCompte of the same County, Gent.: "Discovery" containing 50 a. more
or less. Hanna, wife of William Willowby. Wit: Ralph Blackhall, John Pines.
Acknowledged Jan 2 1671. Ralph Blackhall, Atty for Anthony LeCompte. Edward
Sauvage, Clk.

3 Old 238/Jan 2 1671/William Worgan of Dorchester County, Inholder, to Henry
Turner of the same County, Carpenter: 1/2 of "Worgan's Ch." containing 25 a.
more or less. Elice, wife of Wm Worgan. Wit: Phine. Blackwood, Thomas
Newman, Edward Sauvage. Acknowledged Jan 2 1671. Edward Sauvage, Clk.

3 Old 239/Dec 16 1671/Isaac Hunt of Dorchester County, Planter to Thomas
Taylor of the same County: "Hooton's Neck" on Hungar River containing 50 a.
more or less. Wit: M. Matthews, Stephen Chapman. Acknowledged Jan 2 1670.
Edward Sauvage, Clk.

3 Old 240/Feb 5 1671/Thomas Seamans of Dorchester County, Planter to Joseph
Woodard of the same County, planter: 1/2 of "Clark's Neck" on Shoal Creek
containing 125 a. (1/2 of 250 a). Wit: William Thomas, Edward Sauvage.
Possession delivered Feb 6 1671 in the presence of Thos Scott and Nicholas
Mace. Acknowledged Feb 6 1671. Edward Sauvage, Clk.

3 Old 240/Feb 5 1671/William Worgan of Fishing Creek in Dorchester County,
Inholder to Edward Sauvage of the same County, Clark: "Worgan's Adventure" on
Little Choptank River and Fishing Creek adj land of Robert Harwood and
Worgan's Creek and containing 50 a. more or less. Wit: Stephen Beeson, John
Wakefield, Thos Croft. Acknowledged Feb 6 1671. Edward Sauvage, Clk.

3 Old 242/Feb 6 1671/Henry Turner and William Merchant of Dorchester County
to Richd. Keene of Calvert County, Inholder: "Clarks Outlett" patented to
Daniell Clark Sep 22 1660 on Little Choptank River and Salt Marsh Creek, containing 100 a. more or less. Wit: John Brooke, Philip Shapley, P. Blackwood,
Henry Trippe, Robert Winsmore. Acknowledged Feb 6 1671. Edward Sauvage, Clk.

3 Old 243/Jan 6 1671/Thomas Hooton of Dorchester County, Planter to Thomas
Taylor, Gent. of the same County: "Doggwood Ridge" on Transquakin Bay (Fishing Bay) adj "Hooton's Rest" and containing 100 a. more or less. Mary, wife
of Thomas Hooton. Wit: William Stephens, William Wroughton, Thomas Gilbert.
Acknowledged Jan 5 1671. Certified by William Stephens and William Wroughton.

3 Old 244/Jan 6 1671/Thomas Hooton of Dorchester County, Planter to Thomas
Taylor of the same County: "Hooton's Rest" on Transquakin Bay (Fishing Bay)
and Hooton's Creek, near a parcel of land laid out for William Smith. 100 a.

conveyed. Mary, wife of Thomas Hooton (Hutton). Wit: William Stephens, William Wroughton, Thomas Gilbert. Acknowledged Jan 6 1671. Certified by William Stephens and William Wroughton. Bond witnessed by William Stephens, William Wroughton, Thomas Gilbert, Richard Meekins. Edward Sauvage, Clk.

3 Old 245/Jan 2 1671/Thomas Hooton of Dorchester County, planter to Richard Meekins of the same County: "Hutton's Chance" at the upper end of Tar Bay containing 50 a. more or less. Mary, wife of Thomas Hooton. Wit: William Wroughton, William Stephens, Thomas Gilbert, Thomas Taylor. Acknowledged Jan 6 1671. Certified by William Stephens, William Wroughton and Edward Sauvage, Clk.

3 Old 247/Last day of February, 1671/Thomas Taylor of Dorchester County, High Sheriff to Daniel Holland of the Colony of Virginia, planter: "Taylor's Inheritance" containing 200 a. on an island in St. Johns Creek patented to Thomas Taylor May 29 1668. Frances, wife of Thomas Taylor. Wit: Edward Sauvage. Acknowledged Mar 6 1671. Edward Sauvage, Clk.

3 Old 249/Jan 16 1671/Power of Atty from Ellinor Staplefort to William Dorrington to acknowledge to Daniel Holland 200 a. called "Commencement" sold to Holland by the husband of said Ellinor Staplefort. Wit: John Phillips, James Crosse. Acknowledged Mar 6 1671. Edward Sauvage, Clk.

3 Old 249/Francis Tarsell, planter of Dorchester County to John Bloare of Talbot County, planter: "Tarsells Neck" on the east side of Blackwater in Dorchester County, containing 200 a. more or less. Margaret Tarsell, wife of Francis Tarsell. Wit: Thomas Fisher, Robert Diges. Acknowledged Mar 6 1671. Edward Sauvage, Clk. Bond witnessed by A. Wright, Daniel Clarke.

3 Old 250/Aug 6 1672/Thomas Taylor, Gent. of Dorchester County and Frances his wife to Benjamin Granger, planter of the same County: "Dividing Point" on Little Choptank River containing 100 a. more or less. Acknowledged Aug 6 1672 by Thomas Taylor and Henry Trippe, atty for Frances Taylor. Edward Sauvage, Clk.

3 Old 251/Jun 10 1672/Thomas Oliver of Dorchester County, planter to Samuel Pritchett of the same County, planter: One Moyety of "Humphreys Fortune" on a branch of Fishing Creek containing 150 a. more or less. Susan, wife of Thomas Oliver. Wit: Henry Parker, Peter Stoakes, Henry Beckwith, Anthony Hardacre. Acknowledged Aug 6 1672. Edward Sauvage, Clk.

3 Old 252/Jun 10 1672/Anthony Hardacre of Dorchester County, planter to Peter Stoaks of the same County: One Moyety of "Hailes Choyce" on Fishing Creek, being the eastermost part of said parcel of land. Wit: Henry Parker, Thomas Oliver. Acknowledged Aug 6 1672. Edward Sauvage, Clk.

3 Old 254/Aug 1 1672/Thomas Pratt of Annarundell County to James Agg and William Merchant of Dorchester County: 100 a. called "Congum" granted unto Robert Loyd by patent dated Jul 29 1664 and conveyed to Thomas Pratt by deed dated Dec 2 1665. Ann, wife of Thomas Pratt. Wit: John Hillen, Thos Croft. Acknowledged Aug 6 1672 by Peter Stoakes, Atty for Grantors. Edward Sauvage, Clk.

3 Old 257/Aug 28 1672/John Richardson of Talbot County, planter from Timothy Goodridge of the same County, planter: "Goodridge Choice" on Cabin Creek adj land of William Troath and containing by estimation 600 a. Wit: Simon Warford, William Charlton, Edward Williams. Acknowledged Sep 3 1672. Edward Sauvage, Clk.

3 Old 258/Aug 28 1672/John Rawlings of Dorchester County to John Person of the same County, planter: "Addition" on the NW Branch of Transquakin on the western side, containing 100 a. Wit: Edward Sauvage. Acknowledged Sep 1672. Edward Sauvage, Clk.

3 Old 259/Nov 4 1672/Arthur Wright of Dorchester County, "Taylor" to Anthony Tall Jr of the same County, "Couper": Land on Little Choptank River and Wright's Creek, on the western side of the creek containing 100 a. more or less and called "Wright's Lott." Abigail, wife of Arthur Wright. Acknowledged Nov 5 1672. Edward Sauvage, Clk.

3 Old 260/Oct 29 1672/John Bloare, planter of Talbot County to Alex. Fisher of Dorchester County: "Tarsells Neck" on the east side of Blackwater containing 200 a. more or less. Wit: William Kendall, Theophilus Sacheverell. Acknowledged Nov 5 1672. Edward Sauvage, Clk.

3 Old 261/Nov 4 1672/William Willowby of Dorchester County, "Playsterer" and John Stratton to William Fisher of the same County, planter (Hannah, wife of William Willowby): "Rosewell" ("Roxwell"?) adj land of Anthony LeCompte and containing 50 a. Wit: Robert Staplefort, John Bloar. Acknowledged Nov 5 1672. Edward Sauvage, Clk.

3 Old 262/1672/John Edmondson of Talbot County, Gent. to William Harper (Hays?) of Dorchester County, planter: "Skillington" on Hungar River containing 100 a. more or less. Sarah, wife of John Edmondson. Acknowledged Nov 5 1672 by John Brooke, Atty for Grantor. Bond witnessed by Thomas Gilbert. Power of Atty witnessed by Edward Cook and Rd. Rayner.

3 Old 263/Dec 3 1672/John Edmondson of Talbot County, Merchant to Robert Frances of the same County, planter (Sarah, wife of John Edmondson): "Hogg Point" on Hogg Creek containing 300 a. more or less in all, 200 a. being conveyed. Wit: John Stratton, Geo. Robothom. Acknowledged Dec 3 1672. Edward Sauvage, Clk.

3 Old 264/Dec 3 1672/John Pitts of Talbot County, Merchant to Cuthbert Phelps of the same County, planter (Frances, wife of John Pitts): Land laid out for Thomas Langdon on the south side of Great Choptank River and on Hunting Creek, on the north side of the creek, containing 400 a. more or less. Wit: John Stratton, Peter Baucomb. Acknowledged Dec 3 1672. Peter Baucomb, Atty for Cuthbert Phelps. Edward Sauvage, Clk.

3 Old 265/Jun 3 1671/Henry Hooper of Calvert County, planter to Lewis Griffin of Dorchester County, planter: "Buck Valley" containing 50 a. on a creek running into Transquakin Bay, granted to Hooper by patent dated Jun 8 1669. Wit: Daniel Clark, Robert Winsmore. Acknowledged Dec 3 1672. Edward Sauvage, Clk.

3 Old 267/Jan 30 1672/Thomas Newton of Little Choptank River in Dorchester County, planter to Phineas Blackwood, Schoolmaster of Dorchester County: "Blould (?) Point" at the mouth of Slaughter Creek, on the east side of said creek and on Newton's Cove, containing 100 a. more or less. Wit: Daniel Wilford, William Morgan. Acknowledged Feb 5 1672. Edward Sauvage, Clk.

3 Old 268/Nov 29 1672/Andrew Insley of Dorchester County, Gent. to Richard Meekins of the same County, planter: "Insley's Chance" on Hungar River at Andews marsh, containing 50 a. more or less. Wit: Thomas Gilbert, Richard Cadmore, Daniel Hugill (Hookill). Acknowledged Mar 4 1672. Edward Sauvage, Clk.

4 Old 1/2/Mar 1 1679/William Merchant of Dorchester County, planter to Bartholomew Ennalls: "Merchants Adventure" on Transquakin River, containing 150 a. more or less. Wit: William Smithson, Gournay Crowe, Thomas Flowers. Acknowledged Mar 3 1679/80.

4 Old 1/2/Sep 3 1679/Henry Turner and Abigaill his wife to Thomas Taylor, Gent.: "Quinbrogh" on Transquakin River, adj "Turners Delight." Wit: Benj. Hunt, Thos Gilbert. Acknowledged Sep 3 1679. Assignment of dower interest of Abigaill Turner, relict of Henry Turner, deceased, in the above land, to Thomas Taylor dated Mar 3 1679/80. Witnessed by Henry Howard and William Smithson.

4 Old 1/Mar 3 1679/Phineas Blackwood of Dorchester County, Scrivener to John Pollard of the same County, Gent.: "Cedar Poynt" in the bay behind St. James on the south side of Little Choptank River at the mouth of Slater Creek, containing 100 a. more or less. Wit: John Hungerford, William Watson. Acknowledged Mar 3 1679.

4 Old 3/May 1 1680/Thomas Foulks and Sarah his wife to William Dorrington: Release re property left to Sarah by John Cornelius; Peter Johnson and James his son; and Thomas Fisher the late husband of the said Sarah. Wit: John Willis, William Reese, Thomas Jones. Acknowledged Jun 1 1680.

4 Old 4/May 1 1680/William Dorrington to Thoma Foulkes and Sarah his wife: Release. Wit: John Willis, William Reese, Thomas Jones. Acknowledged Jun 1 1680.

4 Old 4/May 2 1680/William Dorrington to Thomas Foulkes, Chirurgeon: Bill for 14000 pounds of tobacco to be paid by Dorrington to Foulkes. Wit: John Willis, William Reese, Thomas Jones. Acknowledged in open Court Jun 1 1680.

4 Old 4/May 22 1679/William Morgan of the City of Bristol, Merchant to Morris Matthews: Power of Atty. Wit: Lawrence Woodnutt, John Plumer, Simon Stephens. Proved in open Court Jun 1 1680.

4 Old 5/Jun 1 1678/Lemuel Mason of Elizabeth River in the County of Lower Norfolk in Virginia, Gent. to Charles Egerton of the same County: power of Atty to receive property due Mason in the Province of Maryland "and more expecially an Estate Reall & psonall in the hands of Mr. William Dorrington of Great Choptank River in the Province of Maryland aforesaid, which shall appear due to me as marrying Ann Seywell sister & heir to Mr. Henry Sewell deceased." Wit: Joseph Jackson, Wm Porten, Matthew Godfree, Nicholas Williams. Proved Jun 10 1678 by oaths of Joseph Jackson and Nicholas Williams, before Phillip Calvert.

4 Old 5/Oct 3 1672/Deposition of Richard Bennett of Nansemond County, Virginia, re Ann, wife of Col. Lemuel Mason of Lower Norfolk County, Virginia, daughter of Henry Sewell, Merchant, deceased, late of the said County of Norfolk, and sole sister of Mr. Henry Sewell the younger, deceased.

4 Old 6/Apr 16 1672/Depositions of Richard Hargrave, Sr, aged about 60 years, and Simon Peters re Ann, born "about seaven or eight and thrity years since," wife of Col. Lemuel Mason, daughter of Henry Sewell, Merchant and sister of Henry Sewell the younger, late deceased. Copies certified by Herbert Jeffreys, Esq., Governor and Captain General of Virginia, Sep 24 1678 at ".James Citty in Virginia."

4 Old 6/Sep 29 1679/Abigail Wright of Dorchester County, widow, to her children, Grace Wright, Absalom Wright, Edward Williams, Arthur Wright and Naomi Wright: Livestock. Wit: Wm. Stephens, Thomas Taylor, William Smithson. Acknowledged Sep 29 1679.

4 Old 7/May 5 1680/Thomas Cooke to Edward Cooke: gift of all his estate.
Wit: Henry Howard, Peter Stockes, William Thomas. Acknowledged Jun 1 1680 by
Henry Howard, Atty for Thomas Cooke.

4 Old 9/May 5 1680/Thomas Cooke of Dorchester County, Merchant to his brother
Edward Cooke of the same County, Gent.: Power of Atty (mentions plantation
belonging to Thomas Cooke, situate on Blackwater River) Wit: Hen. Howard,
Peter Stoakes, Wm Thomas. Acknowledged Jun 1 1680 by the subscribing witnesses. Bond of Edward Cooke to Thomas Cooke.

4 Old 10/Jun 1 1680/John Curtis and Elizabeth his wife to John Davis and John
Jennett of Dorchester County: "Hampton" containing 250 a. on Hunting Creek
and the south side of Great Choptank River, adj land formerly laid out for
Brett Dallender. Wit: Richard Owen, William Walker. Acknowledged Jun 1 1680.

4 Old 12/Jan 4 1679/William Jump of Talbot County, Carpenter to William
Dossey of Dorchester County, planter: "End of Controversie" on Little Choptank River and Fishing Creek near "Teverton" and containing 200 a. more or
less. Wit: Hen. Howard, Tho. Foulkes, Jno Edwards. Acknowledged Jun 1 1680.

4 Old 14/Jun 1680/Thomas Taylor of Dorchester County to William Travers of
the same County, Merchant: 30 a. on the south side of beaverdam branch which
issues out of the west side of Transquakin River, part of 500 a. in the
occupation of Wm Hill, Merchant. Wit: Hen. Howard, Wm Smithson. Frances,
wife of Thomas Taylor. Acknowledged Jun 2 1680 before Wm Stephens and John
Brooke. Bond from Thomas Taylor to William Travers.

4 Old 16/Feb 24 1679/Thomas Flowers of Dorchester County, planter to John
Pearson of the same place, planter: "Havre de grace" in the fork of Black-
water River containing 100 a. more or less. Wit: Gournay Crowe, Barth.
Ennalls. Acknowledged Mar 3 1679.

4 Old 17/Jun 15 1680/Robert Trusteene to Joseph Searjant: Power of Atty.
Wit: Mary Wiltsheere, Precilla Davis. Proved Aug 3 1680. Wm Stephens, John
Brooke.

4 Old 18/Jun 16 1680/James Love to Joseph Serjant: Power of Atty. Wit: John
Dossey, Rich. Buttwell. Proved Aug 3 1680. Wm Stephens, John Brooke.

4 Old 18/Oct 10 .../Ann Webb to Simon Stephens: Indenture. Wit: Sam Webb.
Ann Webb transported to this province in the ship Sarah & Elizabeth, Richard
White, Master, Apr 25 1680.

4 Old 19/Oct 1 1677/John Holt of Talbot County, Planter to Thomas Colton of
the same County, planter: 300 a. called "Bretts Hope," 1/2 of 600 a. formerly patented to Brett Allender on the south side of Great Choptank River and
Hunting Creek. Wit: John Gordon, James Derumple, Mary Clements.

4 Old 20/Sep 8 1682/Testimony of Thomas Taylor, aged 39 years, former deputy
Surveyor; Samuel Millington, aged 41 years; and Staphen Selus (Zealous) aged
about 55 years, re boundary between land of Henry Hooper and land of his
"Brother," William Chaplin on Hoopers Island, sworn to before Henry Trippe
and Edward Pinder.

4 Old 21/Mar 30 1683/Ann James to John Edwards and Susanna his wife: Indenture of William James, son and only child of said Ann James, to serve as an
apprentice until he reaches age 21. Wit: William Smithson, Benj. Priestley,
John Mackeel.

4 Old 21/Mar 1 1679/William Merchant of Dorchester County to Bartholomew
Ennalls: "Merchants Adventure" on Transquakin River containing 150 a. more or
less. Wit: William Smithson, Gournay Crowe, Thomas Flowers. Acknowledged in

open Court Mar 3 1679/80.

4 Old 21/Sep 3 1679/Henry Turner and Abigall his wife to Thomas Taylor, Gent.: "Quinborough" on west side of Transquakin River adj "Turners Delight." Wit: Benj. Hunt, Thos Gilbert. Acknowledged Sep 3 1679.

4 Old 22/Apr 20 1677/Robert Clarke, son and heir of ___ Clarke late of Calvert County, deceased, to John Edmondson of Talbot County: C... Ridge on Great Choptank River and Fallen Creek, containing 400 a. more or less. Wit: Wm Stephens, John Milles. Acknowledged Apr 21 1677 before Thomas Notley and Phillip Calvert.

4 Old 23/Mar 30 1679/Richard Meekins of Dorchester County to John Meredith, Planter: "Insleys Chance" on Hungar River at Andrews Marsh containing 50 a. more or less; and "Great Waldam" on Hungar River containing 50 a. more or less. Wit: Thomas Pattison, Gournay Crowe. Acknowledged by Joana, wife of Richard Meekins, Nov 3 1680.

4 Old 29/Jan 9 1680/William Dorrington of Dorchester County, Gent. to Daniel Clarke, Henry Trippe and Maurice Matthews, all of Dorchester County, and Francis Dorrington of Calvert County, in consideration of the marriage of William Dorrington and Elizabeth his wife: "Busby" containing 500 a. more or less; "Temple Street" containing 256 a.; "Bowling Greene" containing 19 a. more or less; "Hogshead" containing 100 a. more or less; "Clift" containing 200 a. more or less; and "Clifton" containing 200 a. more or less, 1275 a. in all, in trust for the benefit of said William Dorrington and others, excluding Sarah Dorrington, alias Fisher. William Dorrington of Calvert County, late of the City of Bristol, Cooper, mentioned as kinsman of grantor. Wit: Henry Howard, Robert Masters, Charles Morgin, James Fielding. Acknowledged Aug 3 1681. Thos Smithson, Clk. Deed voided. Sam Smith, Clk.

4 Old 30/Mar 14 1680/Edward Newton of Dorchester County, son and heir of Thomas Newton deceased, to John Woodward of the City of Bristol, Merchant: "Papaw Tickett" on Little Choptank River, Fishing Creek and Teverton Creek, containing 150 a. by estimation. Also "Papa Thicket Poynt" containing 50 a. Wit: Thos Pattison, Thos Smithson. Acknowledged before Thos Taylor and John Brooke. Thos Smithson, Clk.

4 Old 31/Jan 3 1681/George Sillivan of Minehead, Somerset, England, Mariner, to John Newton of Dorchester County: Power of Atty. Wit: Peter Stoakes, James Agg. Acknowledged Jan 3 1681. Thomas Smithson, Clk.

4 Old 32/John Woodward and Maurice Mathews to Edward Newton: Bond. Wit: Thos Pattison, Thos Smithson. Acknowledged before Thos Taylor, John Brooke.

4 Old 33/May 17 1681/John Hungerford to Alexander Dennett: Assignment of 23 servants. Wit: John Pollard, Benj. Priestley. Proved in open Court Dec 6 1681. Thomas Smithson, Clk.

4 Old 33/Dec 1 1679/Andrew Insley of Dorchester County, planter, to William Tapticoe of the same place, planter: "Andrews Cove" on the east side of Hunger River, on the north side of the east branch of Fox Creek which issues out of said river; 100 a. more or less to be held of the Manor of Nanticoke. Elizabeth, wife of Andrew Insley. Wit: George Ferguson, John Jefferson. Acknowledged Oct 18 1681. Thomas Smithson, Clk. Henry Hooper, Atty for William Tapticoe. Power of Atty dated Oct 18 1681 and witnessed by William Travers, Thomas Travers.

4 Old 35/Jun 28 1681/Alexander Dennett to John Pollard: Power of Atty. Wit: Benj. Priestley. Proved Oct 18 1681. Thomas Smithson, Clk.

4 Old 36/Oct 18 1681/Last Will and Testament of Thomas Seamans: To his wife, Priscilla Seamans, 1/2 of testator's dwelling plantation called "Clerkes :! Neck," and personal property. To his son James Seamans, the remaining 1/2 of "Clerkes Neck." Also mentions his sons John Seamans of New England and Thomas Seamsns. Wit: Gournay Crowe, H. Hubbert, Hen. Howard. Acknowledged Oct 18 1681. Thomas Smithson, Clerk.

4 Old 36/Oct 18 1681/John Plummer of Dorchester County, "Taylor," to William Willowby of the same County, planter: "Buttwells Choice" near the head of Little Choptank River adj land of Robert Winsmore and containing 100 a. more or less. Wit: William Dossey. Acknowledged Oct 18 1681 by John Plummer and Mary his wife. Thomas Smithson, Clk.

4 Old 37/Oct 20 1680/"Recd. ye 20th day of October, 1680 of Edward Pindar Admr. of all & singular ye goods & chattels rights & credits wch were of William Ford of Dorchester County deceased by me James Derumple who maryed wth Mary Clements adm. of all & singular ye goods & chattels rights & credits wch were of John Clements deceased the full & just sum of ten thousand pounds of tobb. it being in full for a bond of one hundred & forty pounds sterling for payment of seaventy pounds sterling, from the said William Ford to ye said John Clements, bearing date the first day of December 1674 which said bond is now in ye possession of Christopher Rousby my attourney at law, the which I doe engage to deliver up to the said Edward Pindar or his order upon demand In wittness whereof I hereunto sett my had & seale the day & year above sd.
James Derumple"
Witnessed by Wm Smithson and Richard Owen.

4 Old 38/Oct 18 1681/William Willoby to John Plummer: "Willoby's Purchase" on Johns Creek adj land of John Stephens & containing 100 a. more or less. Wit: William Dossey. Acknowledged by William Willoby and Hannah hiw wife Oct 18 1681. Thomas Smithson, Clk.

4 Old 39/Oct 18 1680/Benjamin Hunt of Dorchester County to Philadelphia Rawlins of the same place: "Masons Hopyard" on Transquakin River containing 150 a. more or less. Wit: William Smithson, Hen. Howard.

4 Old 40/Mar 1 1680/Robert Dix of Dorchester County, planter to John Stephens: "Roberts Chance" on a beaverdam branch of Blackwater River containing 50 a. more or less. Elizabeth, wife of Robert Dix.

4 Old 41/Dec 3 1681/William Dorrington of Dorchester County, Gent. to William Wanchlow, John Stephens and Maurice Mathews: 1000 a. more or less on Blackwater. Elizabeth, wife of William Dorrington. Wit: Robert Masters, Nathan Jones, Griff. Jones. Acknowledged Dec 7 1681. Thos Smithson, Clk.

4 Old 43/Jan 3 1681/Edward Newton and Maurice Mathews, planters of Dorchester County, to Thomas Mitchell, Merchant of the City of Cork, Ireland: Bond. Wit: Petter Stoakes; James Agge. Acknowledged Jan 3 1681.

4 Old 44/Dec 7 1681/Samuel Millington of Dorchester County, planter to Thomas Banckes of Calvert County, Admr. of George Beckwith deceased: "Millington's Hope" containing 100 a. more or less, on a branch of Transquakin River called Blackwater. Charles Beckwith, son and heir of George Beckwith deceased. Wit: Gournay Crowe, William Smithson. Acknowledged Dec 7 1681 by Samuel Millington and Gournay Crowe, Atty for Ruth Millington, wife of Samuel Millington, before Thomas Taylor and Barth. Ennalls.

4 Old 46/Nov 1 1681/Henry Parker of Talbot County to William Warner of Dorchester County: "Hoggpen Neck" containing 100 a. more or less. Acknowledged Dec 6 1681. Thomas Smithson, Clk.

4 Old 48/Feb 2 1681John Tench to William Willoby: "Bridge North" on the north side of Little Choptank River on the west side of Hudsons Creek, containing 50 a. Wit: William Smithson, Thomas Smithson.

4 Old 49/Feb 16 1680/Henry Orton of Calvert County, planter to Francis Twiford of Dorchester County: "Winfield Trouble" (in Little Choptank) devised to Orton by John Winfield of Calvert County in his Last Will and Testament dated Feb 20 1678/9. Wit: Jonas Winfield, Thos Walmsley. Acknowledged Dec 7 1681 by John Brooke, Atty for Henry Orton.

4 Old 50/Dec 6 1681/Edward Newton to James Peterkin: Bond re division of 1000 a. called "Partnership" on Transquakin River, to be made by Thomas Pattison, Deputy Surveyor, 500 a. to Newton and 500 a. to Peterkin. Wit: William Tregoe, Sr., Hen. Howard. Acknowledged Dec 6 1681. Thomas Smithson, Clk.

4 Old 50/Dec 6 1681/James Peterkin to Edward Newton: Bond re division of 1000 a. called "Partnership" on Transquakin. Wit: William Tregoe, Sr., Hen. Howard. Acknowledged Dec 6 1681. Thomas Smithson, Clk.

4 Old 50/Feb 4 1671/Philip Shapley to Thos Coulton of Northumberland County, Virginia: Bond re sale of 100 a. on Hungar River, near the mouth of the river, sold by Shapley to Coulton. Wit: Charles Hutchins, John Bates. Proved Dec 6 1681. Thos Smithson, Clk.

4 Old 51/Aug 4 1681/Edward Pindar to John Plummer: "Buttwells Choyce" near the head of Little Choptank River adj land of Robert Winsmore and containing 100 a. more or less. Wit: William Smithson, Thomas Smithson. Acknowledged Aug 4 1681 before William Stephens and John Brookes.

4 Old 51/Feb 7 1681/Henry Aldred of Dorchester County to William Marchant: "Stow," on the south side of Southeys beaverdam branch of Blackwater River, adj "Hereford" and containing 16 a. more or less. Wit: Thomas Pattison, Edw. Cooke. Mary Aldred, wife of Henry Aldred. Acknowledged Mar 7 1681/2. Thos Smithson, Clk.

4 Old 53/Feb 7 1681/Henry Aldred to James Harle of Dorchester County, planter: "Beelow" on the east side of Hudsons beaverdam branch of Blackwater River, containing 50 a. more or less. Wit: Thos Pattison, Edw. Cooke. Mary Aldred, wife of Henry Aldred. Acknowledged Mar 7 1681. Thos. Smithson, Clk.

4 Old 53/Jul 4 1682/William Walker of Dorchester County, planter to Mikell Wayte of the same County, planter: 1/2 of a parcel of land called "Blenthhorne Poynt," containing 200 a. Wit: William Wattson, Thos Taylor. Acknowledged Aug 3 1682. Thos Smithson, Clk.

4 Old 54/Jan 6 1681/William Walker to Thomas Taylor: 100 a. called "Guttridge Choice" sold to Walker by William Troth. Wit: Thos Colton, William Watson. Acknowledged Jan 6 1681. Thomas Smithson, Clk.

4 Old 54/Aug 1 1682/Benjamin Hunt of Dorchester County, Gent. to William Tregore, Jr. of the same County, Mariner: "Strawberry Garden" on the NW branch of Transquakin River, on the west side of the river, adj Michll. Mason's land and containing 150 a. more or less. Wit: Hen. Howard, Thos Smithson. Acknowledged Aug 4th. Thos. Smithson, Clk.

4 Old 55/Mary 18 1682/John Edmondson of Talbot County, Atty for Mary Phillips the wife of Thomas Phillips, deceased, to George Alomby of the same county:

"Poyny Poynt" on Hogg Creek, containing 250 a. more or less. Wit: Edward Hargreave, Francis Sutton.

4 Old 57/Sep 10 1666/Patent to Robert Blinkhorne for transporting John Clarke, Jane Wanckling, Jeremiah Monmee(?) and Lewis Stephens to this province as settlers: 200 a. called "Blinkhornes Poynt" on the south side of : Great Choptank River adj land laid out for Timothy Goodridge, and bounded on the west by Hunton Creek. Conveyed by Blinkhorne to William Walker of Dorchester County, planter, Jul 16 1681. Wit: Francis Gill, Thomas Flowers. Power of Atty from Robert Blinkhorne and Bridgett his wife, both of Calvert County, to Thomas Pattison to acknowledge above land to William Walker, dated Jun 1 1682 and witnessed by John Smith and William Brice.

4 Old 58/Mar 20 1681/William Stafford of Dorchester County from George Forgeson of the same county: "Betty's Lot" containing 100 a. more or less on Fox Creek and Hungar River. Wit: John Hungerford, George Hooper. Acknowledged Jun 6 1682. Thos. Smithson, Clk.

4 Old 58/Jun 7 1682/John Pritchett of Dorchester County, planter to John Hungerford of the same County: "Ringwood" containing 50 a. on the east side of Hungar River and on the north side of a small bay called Rehoby Bay, granted to John Pritchett Nov 14 1681. Wit: Thos Pattison, Gournay Crowe.

4 Old 59/Mar 9 1682/Miles Gibson and Ann his wife of Baltimore County to William Troth of Talbot County: 300 a. formerly patented to Thomas Thurston of Jan 10 1667, on the south side of the head of Ingrams Creek. Wit: Thomas Smith, Daniell Lawrence. Acknowledged Mar 31 1682 by Ann Gibson before George Wells and John Waterson. Acknowledged Nov 7 1682 by Samuel Hatton before William Stephens and Thomas Taylor.

4 Old 61/Jun 3 1682/Thomas Colton to John Nicholls: 125 a., part of 300 a. which is 1/2 of 600 a. laid out for Brett Dallender on the south side of Hunting Creek. Mary, wife of Thomas Colton. Wit: Anthony Squire, William Cheesman.

4 Old 62/Sep 5 1682/Agreement between Wm Merchant and James Harte re plantation of Marchant on Blackwater River. Wit: Edward Pindar, John Hudson, Benj. Hunt. Acknowledged in open Court Nov 8 1682. Thomas Smithson, Clk.

4 Old 63/Oct 10 1682/John Phillips to Henry Hooper, Gentleman: "Orphans Increase" on the east side of Worlds End Creek that issues out of Hungar River, containing 50 a. more or less. Signed by John Phillips and Mary Phillips. Wit: William Travers, John Hungerford.

4 Old 64/Aug 30 1684/Thomas Pattison of James Island to Peter Perry of Dorchester County, planter: 50 a. called "Sandish" on the north side of a beaverdam branch of the northwest branch of Blackwater River. Ann Pattison, wife of Thomas Pattison. Wit: Phine. Blackwood, James Pattison. Acknowledged Jan 6 1684/5. Thomas Smithson, Clk.

4 Old 65/Aug 4 1684/William Travers of Dorchester County, Gent. to Bartholomew Ennalls of the same County, Gent.: 30 a. on a beaverdam branch of Transquakin River; also a parcel of land called "Traverses Lott" on the north side of Chicamocomico or Phillips Creek, containing 300 a. more or less; also "Traverses Addition" on a beaverdam branch of Transquakin River containing 50 a. more or less. Wit: Thomas Pattison, Henry Symons, John Capps. Acknowledged in open Court Aug 6 1684. Thomas Smithson, Clk.

4 Old 66/Jun 7 168-/Anthony Squire of Dorchester County, Cooper and Alice
his wife and William Carr of the same County, planter to Joseph Wiggott of
Talbott County: 100 a. of "Goodridges Choyce" conveyed by Goodridge to Wm
Troth, conveyed by Troth to Wm Walker, conveyed by Walker to Thos Taylor,
conveyed by Taylor to the said Anthony Squire and William Carr. Wit: John
Nicolls, Delahay, John Davis, John Wade, William Watson. Acknowledged Aug 24
1687 before John Brookes and Henry Hoopson.

4 Old 68/Jun 8 1687/Thomas Smithson late of Dorchester County and Thomas
Smithson of Talbot County, Gent. to Thomas Hicks and Jeremiah Davis: "Seckter"
containing 769 a. more or less on a branch of Chicacomoco River; and "Cambre
Lake" adj "Seckter," containing 100 a. more or less. Wit: John Hodson,
Francis Anderton. Signed and acknowledged by Thomas Smithson (Sr.) of Talbot
County and John Taylor, Atty for Thomas Smithson late of Dorchester County.
Acknowledged before John Brooke and John Woodward. Thomas Pattison, Clk.

4 Old 69/Feb 27 1689/90/John Jones of Dorchester County, Carpenter, to his
brother William Jones of Dorchester County, planter: Grantor's interest in
two tracts at the head of Hungar River, containing about 200 a., belonging to
William Jones, deceased father of grantor at the time of his death and now in
the possession of grantor's mother and father in law, John Kembell. Wit:
William Travers, Mathew Travers, Roger Clark.

4 Old 70/Jan 23 1689/90/Grace Barnes, wife of John Barnes of Dorchester
County, to Benjamin Hunt of the same County: Power of Atty to acknowledge
deed for 1750 a. called "Martins Hundred" on Nanticoke River, sold by said
John Barnes to Mr. Henry Hooper. Wit: William Hill, John Sharpe. Proved
Mar 4 1689/90 before Henry Trippe and John Brooke. Thomas Pattison, Clk.

4 Old 70/Jan 20 1689/90/James Nowell of Dorchester County, planter and Mar-
garet his wife to John Harwood of the same County, carpenter: "Nowells
Pokety" called "Chance" formerly laid out for Anthony LeCompte. Wit: Phill.
Pitt, Margaret Bleth. Acknowledged Mar 4 1689/90 before Henry Trippe and
John Brooke. Thomas Pattison, Clk.

4 Old 71/Mar 4 1689/90/Henry Eliot and Ann Eliot his wife to Thomas Cooke:
Power of Atty to acknowledge to Arthur Whitely a deed dated Mar 5 1688/89 for
50 a. called "Henry's Choyce." Wit: Thomas Pattison, Robert S... Proved Mar
4 1689/90 before Henry Trippe and John Brooke. Thomas Pattison, Clk.

4 Old 71/Mar 5 1688/89/Henry Eliot of Dorchester County, planter to Arthur
Whitely, Inholder: "Henry's Choyce" adj lands of William Worgan and Daniel
Jones at the head of Fishing Creek in Little Choptank River, containing 50 a.
more or less. Wit: Thomas Pattison, Robert Scrich(?) Acknowledged by Thomas
Cooke, Atty for Henry Eliot and Ann his wife, Mar 4 1689/90 before Henry
Trippe and John Brooke. Thomas Pattison, Clk.

4 Old 72/Jun 4 1690/Abigale Davis, Edward Williams and Abigale Adams to
Maurice Mathews, all of Dorchester County: land formerly pruchased by Arthur
Wright, deceased, husband and father in law of grantors, from John Stuart,
also deceased, containing 50 a., being part of 350 a. patented to said Stuart;
also "Hodsons Point" on Stuarts Creek patented to Arthur Wright Feb 6 1667
and containing 100 a. more or less; also "Crick" patented to Arthur Wright
Sep 9 1675 and containing 66 a. more or less. Wit: Thomas Pattison. Acknowledged Jun 4 1690 before John Brooke and Jacob Loockerman. Thomas Pattison,
Clk.

4 Old 74/Jun 4 1689/Thomas Killman of Dorchester County, planter to Henry
Mitchell of Calvert County, Gent.: "Long Point" on James Island containing

200 a. Wit: Jacob Loockerman, Thos Pattison. Acknowledged Jun 4 1690 before John Brooks and Jacob Loockerman. Thomas Pattison, Clk.

4 Old 75/May 1 1690/Partnership agreement between John Gooty Sr of Dorchester County, Tanner, and Michaell Todd of Dorchester County, "shoemaker alias cordwinder." Wit: John Coale, John Birely. Acknowledged Jun 5 1690 before Charles Huchins and Jacob Loockerman. Thomas Pattison, Clk.

4 Old 76/May 13 1690/Margarett Gautier, wife of John Gautier Sr, to Thomas Cooke: Power of Atty to acknowledge deed for three parcels of land on Blackwater sold by John Gautier Sr to John Gautier, son of said Margarett (Marguerit) Gautier. Wit: John Coale, John C..., Michaell Todd. Proved Jun 5 1690 before Charles Huchins and Jacob Loockerman. Thomas Pattison, Clk.

4 Old 77/Jun 2 1684/Thomas Foulkes, Chirurgeon of Dorchester County to i William Watson, planter, of the same County: " Foulkes Content" containing 100 a., adj land sold by Wm Dorrington to Thomas Fisher. Wit: Richard Owen, William Greene. Acknowledged Aug 6 1684. Thomas Smithson, Clk.

4 Old 78/Apr 4 1667/Stephen Gary of Little Choptank in Talbot County, Mariner, to John Pollard of "Pottuxent" in Calvert County, Cooper: 750 a. on the south side of Little Choptank Creek, on the bay behind St. James Island, patented to Gary the last day of Feb 1662. Wit: John Hudson, Robert Turner, John alford. Clare Gary, wife of Stephen Gary. Acknowledged Jun 8 1682. Thomas Smithson, Clk.

4 Old 80/May 1 1683/John Southy of Dorchester County, planter to John Button of the same county, Cooper: Release. Wit: Thomas Faulkes, William Smithson. Acknowledged Jun 5 1683. Thomas Smithson, Clk.

4 Old 80/May 1 1683/John Button to John Southy: Release. Wit: William Smithson, Thomas Foulkes. Acknowledged Jun 5 1683. Thomas Smithson, Clk.

4 Old 80/Jun 5 1683/John Southy to John Button; and John Button to John Southy: deeds and bonds re division of a tract of 100 a. called "Turkey Poynt" purchased by Southy and Button from John Hudson on the west side of Blackwater adj land of William Jones. Land on the western side of Hudsons branch conveyed to Button, and lasd on the eastern side of Hudsons branch conveyed to Southy. Wit: Thomas Foulkes, William Smithson. Acknowledged in open Court Jun 5 1683 - Aug 5 1683. Thos Smithson, Clk. Mary Button, wife of John Button.

4 Old 84/Nov 28 1683/Thomas Foulkes of Dorchester County, Gent. to John Baker of St. Mary's County, Gent.; 250 a. called "Foulkes Delight" on the north side of the east branch of Hunting Creek which issues out of the south side of Great Choptank River. Wit: Benj. Hunt, Thomas Wall. Acknowledged Nov 29 1683. Thomas Smithson, Clk. Bond dated Nov 7 1683, witnessed by John Barnes, William Holland, Geo. Curwen.

4 Old 86/Feb 3 1679/Thomas Sumers of Dorchester County, planter to John Merydith of the same county, planter: "Tuksbury" on the east side of Charles Creek which issues out of Hungar River, containing 50 a. more or less. Wit: Henry Hooper, William Travers, Phillip Ahearne, John Phillips. Acknowledged Feb 10 1679/Signed by Thomas Sumers and Mary Sumers.

4 Old 87/Aug 2 1682/John Causey of Dorchester County, planter to John Hudson of the same County, planter: "Causeys Lott" on the west side of Chicamocomico River, containing 100 a. more or less. Wit: William Smithson, Benj. Hunt. Acknowledged Aug 2 1682. Henry Trippe, John Brooke. Bond witnessed by Benj. Hunt, Wm Trego Junr.

4 Old 88/Jan 28 1681/2/John Haslewood to William Evans: Livestock. Wit: Gload Lewis, John Lewis.

4 Old 88/Jun 3 1682/Thomas Colton to John Nicolls: Bond for conveyance of 125 a. of a tract of 600 a. called "Bretts Hope," from Colton to Nicolls. Wit: Antho. Squires, William Cheeseman. Acknowledged Dec 5 1682. Thomas Smithson, Clk.

4 Old 89/Aug 1 1682/Thomas Smithson of Dorchester County, Clk. to Benj. Hunt of the same county, planter: "Kipplin" on Chicamocomico River, containing 150 a. more or less. Wit: William Tregoe Junr., Henry Howard.

4 Old 89/Dec 4 1682/John Jones to Edward Booker of Liverpool: Indenture to serve for 4 years in return for transportation to Virginia or Maryland. Signed by Edward Booker. Wit: Edw. Tarleton Major, Thomas Sandiford.

4 Old 90/Dec 25 1682/Daniel Jones to Thomas Hackett: lease of "Riccarton" containing 100 a., for four years. Wit: John Richardson, Obadiah King.

4 Old 90/Oct 9 1682/Joseph Stanaway to Andrew Insley: Bond re sale of two parcels of land by Stanaway to Insley. Wit: George Forgeson, Hugh Syrtherfield, Elinor Styth. Jun 4 1684 - Receipt from John Taylor, Sheriff, for 3 shillings from Andrew Insley for alienation of 100 a.

4 Old 91/Oct 30 1682/Thomas Pattison of Dorchester County to William Evans of the same county: bond for conveyance of "Rye,"Containing 100 a. on Tedious Creek, from Pattison to Evans. Wit: William Safford, Jeffery Meanely.

4 Old 91/Mar 7 1682/Thomas Pattison of Dorchester County, Wine coop, to William Evans of the same County, planter: "Rye,"containing 100 a. more or less, on Tedious Creek. Wit: John Hungerford, Henry Howard. Ann Pattison, wife of Thomas Pattison. Acknowledged Mar 7 1682. Thomas Smithson, Clk.

4 Old 93/Mar 6 1682/John Brooke of Dorchester County, Chirurgeon to Christopher Waller of the same County, planter: "Haslewood" on the western side of the northwest branch of Transquakin River, containing 200 a. more or less. Wit: Anthony Dawson, Henry Howard. Acknowledged Mar 7 1682. Thomas Smithson, Clk.

4 Old 94/Feb 7 1682/Francis Twifford to Thomas Taylor: "Whinfells Trouble" containing 200 a. by estimation. Wit: William Dyer, John Phillips. Acknowledged Feb 7 1682. Thomas Smithson, Clk.

4 Old 95/Mar 7 1682/Thomas Pattison of Dorchester County, wine coop to Jeffery Mainley (Meanely) of the same County, planter: three tracts on the western side of Blackwater River. "Biggen" containing 50 a. more or less; "Barbadoes" containing 50 a. more or less; and "Bull Poynt" on Bohemia Creek, containing 70 a. more or less. Acknowledged Mar 7 1682. Thomas Smithson, Clk. Wit: John Hunberford, Henry Howard. Ann wife of Thomas Pattison.

4 Old 96/Jun 5 1683/John Button of Dorchester County, Cooper, from John Southey of the same county, planter: 50 a. called "Woolverton" laid out for said Button and Southey on Blackwater River, adj a trace called "Hereford" formerly laid out for William Jones; also adj a tract called "Turkey Poynt." Wit: Thomas Foulkes, William Smithson. Acknowledged Jun 5 1683. Thomas Smithson, Clk.

4 Old 96/Jun 5 1683/John Button to John Southey: Bond re division of "Turkey Poynt" jointly purchased by Button and Southy. Wit: William Smithson, Thomas Foulkes. Acknowledged Jun 5 1683. Thomas Smithson, Clk.

4 Old 97/Jan 3 1683/John Edmondson of Talbot County, Merchant and Sarah his wife to James Murphey, Gent.: "Conquericus Fields" on Phillips Creek, adj land of William Parrott and containing 600 a. Wit: Griff. Jones, John Stanley. Acknowledged Jun 5 1683 before Henry Trippe and Edward Pindar. William Smithson, atty for Sarah Edmondson. Receipt for alienation of above land. William Smithson, Sherr.

4 Old 98/Nov 9 1683/William Parratt of Talbot County, planter and Sarah his wife to Thomas Harvy: 100 a. of 1050 a. called "Edmondson's Reserve" in Dorchester County. Wit: Benjamin Parrat, George Haile. Acknowledged Nov 27 1683 by James Benson, atty for William Parratt, before John Brooke and Edward Pindar.

4 Old 99/Nov 7-26 1683/John Dossey, planter of Little Choptank in Dorchester County to Daniell Willard of the same place, planter: Lease of "Old Field" being part of "Preston" on the east side of Little Choptank, for the lifetime of said Willard and if he should died leaving a widow, then the widow to have the use of the land for two years after his death. Wit: Henry Davice, Andrew Prewitt. Acknowledged Nov 29 1683. Thomas Smithson, Clk.

4 Old 99/Oct 13 1682/James Murphey of Talbot County, planter, and Mary his wife, daughter of Richard Richardson deceased and sister and heir of George Richardson deceased, to John Edmondson of Talbot County, Merchant: "Richardson's Folly," formerly known as "Richardson's Clift," containing 750 a. more or less. Wit: Richard Royston, Lewis Blangy. Acknowledged Jun 1683 before Vincent Lowe.

4 Old 100/Nov 28 1683/William Trego of Dorchester County, Mariner to Thomas Oliver and William Marchant: "Refuge" on the northwest branch of Transquakin River, on the west side of the river, adj "Strawberry Garden" and containing 50 a. more or less. Wit: Benjamin Priestley, John LeCompte. Acknowledged Nov 28 1683.

4 Old 101/Jan 11 1683/Thomas Walker of Kent County in Pennsylvania and Sarah his wife to Anthony Dawson of Dorchester County, Carpenter: 1/2 of "Alexanders Place" on Transquakin River containing 650 a., lease for 1000 years. Wit: John Taylor, Thomas Smithson. Acknowledged Jan 11 1683/4 before John Brooke and Bartholomew Ennalls.

4 Old 101/Jan 2 1684/William Marchant of Dorchester County, planter to John Button of the same County, cooper: part of "Hereford" on Blackwater River formerly sold by William Ford deceased, being that part of "Hereford" on the west side of Hudson's Branch. Wit: Thomas Smithson, James Harle. Acknowledged Feb 10 1684 before Thomas Taylor and John Brooke.

4 Old 103/Dec 6 1684/John Haines of Dorchester County, planter to Humphrey Mould of the same county, planter: tract of land containing 22 1/2 a. more or less. Wit: Edward Tench, Edward Wilson. Acknowledged Dec 6 1684 before John Brooke and Bartholomew Ennalls.

4 Old 103/Aug 4 1684/William Greene of Dorchester County, planter ot his daughter Elizabeth Greene: "Partners Choyce" on Nanticoke River and Barren Creek, containing 250 a.; also a tract adj "Partners Choyce" and also containing 250 a. Wit: Thomas Daniell, Sherry Wansie. Acknowledged Aug 5 1684. Thomas Smithson, Clk.

4 Old 103/Aug 4 1684/William Travers of Dorchester County, Gent. to Bartholomew Ennalls of the same County, Gent.: 30 a. more or less on Transquakin River; also "Traverses Lott" on the north side of Chiccanocomoco or Phillips Creek, containing 300 a. more or less; also "Traverses Addition" on a branch

of Transquakin River adj "Traverses Lott" and containing 50 a. more or less. Wit: Thomas Pattison, Henry Simons, John Capps. Acknowledged Aug 6 1684. Thomas Smithson, Clk. Alienation money paid. John Taylor, Sherr.

4 Old 105/Aug 5 1684/Thomas Seamans of Dorchester County to Matthew Hood of the same County: "Addition to Clarkes Neck" on the south side of Little Choptank River, adj land of Nicholas Masey, also adj "Clarkes Neck" and containing 13 a. more or less. Wit: William Hill, Benjamin Hunt. Acknowledged Aug 5 1684. Thomas Smithson, Clk.

4 Old 105/Aug 4 1684/Elizabeth Travers to Henry Hooper: Power of Atty to acknowledge "Traverses Lott" and "Traverses Addition" to Bartholomew Ennalls. Wit: James Moadsley, Elizabeth Moadsley. Proved by witnesses in open Court Aug 6 1684. Thomas Smithson, Clk.

4 Old 106/Dec 13 1683/Robert Evans of Talbot County, planter ot John Davis and Susanna his wife: 1/2 of "Poplar Ridge" on the south side of Hog Island Creek. Penelope, wife of Robert Evans. Wit: Thomas Colton, Stephen Winn, Mary Colton. Acknowledged Aug 5 1684. Thomas Smithson, Clk.

4 Old 107/Jun 2 1684/Thomas Wall of Dorchester County, Inholder to John Foster of the County: "Broken Wharfe" on a branch of the head of Transquakin River, containing 50 a. more or less. Wit: John Hungerford, Benjamin Preistley. Acknowledged Aug 5 1684. Thomas Smithson, Clk.

4 Old 108/1684/John Edmondson of Talbot County, Merchant to Thomas Wall of Dorchester County, Innholder: livestock in the possession of Henry Elliott, formerly sold to Edmondson by William Trego Senr. of Bristol, England, mariner. Wit: Arthur Whitely, Henry Howard. Acknowledged Aug 6 1684. Thomas Smithson, Clk.

4 Old 108/Jun 4 1684/John Edmondson of Talbot County to Thomas Wall of Dorchester County, Innholder: 1/2 of "Worgans Chance" formerly purchased by Edward Sauvage from Thomas Taylor, containing 25 a.; also 50 a. on the south side of Fishing Creek; also the other half of "Worgans Chance;" also Worgans Adventure" containing 50 a. on Little Choptank River and the eastern side of Fishing Creek adj land of Robert Harwood. Tracts formerly purchased by Edmondson from William Tregoe. Wit: Arthur Whiteley, Henry Howard. Acknowledged Aug 6 1684. Thomas Smithson, Clk.

4 Old 110/Jun 2 1684/John Newton of Dorchester County, carpenter to Thomas Wall of the same County, Innholder: "Westminster" between the branches of Transquakin and Chiccanocomocco Rivers, containing 100 a. more or less. Wit: Gournay Crowe, Benj. Priestley. Acknowledged Aug 6 1684. Thomas Smithson, Clk.

4 Old 111/Jan 1 1683/Phillip Williams of Dorchester County, planter and Mary Williams his wife to Henry Harman of the same County, coop.: "Pilgrims Rest" on the east side of Davis Creek which issues out of the north side of Slaughter Creek in Taylors Island, containing 50 a. Wit: Henry Howard, Benj. Priestley. Acknowledged Aug 5 1684 before John Alford and Edward Pindar.

4 Old 112/May 31 1684/Richard Kendall of Dorchester County to Thomas Wroughton: "Kendalls Chance" on Charles Creek in Dorchester County, containing 50 a. more or less. Elizabeth Kendall, wife of Richard Kendall. Wit: George Hooper, John Meredith. Acknowledged Jun 4 1684. Thomas Smithson, Clk.

4 Old 112/Apr 24 1684/William Wattson to Thomas Taylor: "Plaines" containing 300 a. at the head of Hunting Creek adj "Hunting Fields" now in the possession of John Alford, also adj land of Nicholas Painter; also "Watsons Lott" on

the south side of the main branch of Hunting Creek, containing 100 a. by estimation. Wit: Andrew jray, Sarah P... Acknowledged Aug 5 1684. Thomas Smithson, Clk.

4 Old 113/Nov 4 1684/William Borne of Dorchester County, carpenter to Richard Tubman of the same County, planter: "Poolehead" on the east side of Slaughter Creek, containing 200 a. more or less, patented to Richard Meekins Jan 10 1670. Wit: William Hill, Gour. Crow, John Hanes. Acknowledged Nov 4 1684. Thomas Smithson, Clk.

4 Old 114/Jun 10 1684/Rowland Robison and Elizabeth his wife of Talbot County, planter to Thomas Watkinson (Watkins): 140 a. called "Rollands Plain" at the head of Cabin Creek. Wit: Edw. Sydenham, Will Ballfour. Acknowledged Oct 15 1685. Thomas Smithson, Clk.

4 Old 115/Feb 11 1684/5/Thomas Wall of Dorchester County, Innholder to John Ross of the said County and to the children of the first wife of said John Ross: "Jump's Poynt" on the north side of Little Choptank River and the eastern branch of Hudsons Creek, containing 100 a. more or less. Wit: Benj. Priestley, Thomas Veitch. Acknowledged Feb 11 1684/5; Alice Wall, wife of Thomas Wall. Thomas Smithson, Clk.

4 Old 116/Nov 4 1684/William Bourne (Borne) of Dorchester County, Turner to James Moadsley of the same County, planter: "Peaknell" on the eastern side of Slaughter Creek containing 200 a. more or less; also "Bournes Landing" on the southern side of Slaughter Creek and Bournes Creek, containing 100 a. more or less; also "Bournes Conclusion" on the north side of the head of Keenes Beaver Dam Branch which issues out of the south side of Slaughter Creek, containing 100 a. more or less near land called "Polehead." Wit: Richard Meekins, Thos. Smithson. Acknowledged Nov 4 1684. Thomas Smithson, Clk.

4 Old 117/Nov 4 1684/Thomas Taylor of Dorchester County, planter to John Mickall (MacKall) of the same County, "Taylor": "Sandwich" on the north side of Cabin Creek, adj "Milland" and containing 100 a. more or less. Wit: Hum. Hubbert, Anthony Squires. Acknowledged Nov 4 1684. Thomas Smithson, Clk. Alienation money paid Nov 5 1684. John. Taylor Sherr.

4 Old 118/Oct 15 1684/Thomas Taylor to Henry Griffith of Dorchester County, planter: "Watsons Lott" on a branch of Hunting Creek adj "Squires Chance" and containing 100 a. more or less. Wit: Hum. Hubert, Anthony Squires. Acknowledged Nov 4 1684. Thomas Smithson, Clk.

4 Old 119/Nov 4 1684/John Pearson of Dorchester County, planter to Mary Marchant, daughter of William Marchant of the same County, planter: "Havre de grace" in the fork of Blackwater River in Dorchester County, containing 100 a. more or less. Wit: Thomas Smithson, Gournay Crowe. Acknowledged Nov 4 1684. Thomas Smithson, Clk. Receipt for alienation. Jno. Taylor High Sherr. by William Hill, sub Sherr.

4 Old 120/Nov 4 1684/William Walker of Dorchester County, planter to Joseph Wiggott of Talbot County: Part of "Walkers Lott" on Hunting Creek, containing 200 a. more or less. Wit: Thomas Smithson, Jeremiah Smith. Acknowledged Feb 10 1684/5. Thomas Smithson, Clk.

4 Old 121/Aug 1685/William Trego, Jr to Henry Howard: "Strawberry Garden" on the northwest branch of Transquakin River, adj Michaell Mason's land and containing 150 a. more or less. Wit: John Pope, William Lowe. Acknowledged Aug 4 1685 by John Brookes, Atty for William Trego. Thomas Smithson, Clk. Power

of Atty witnessed by Anthony Dawson and John Atkins, dated Jul 22 1684 and proved Aug 4 1685. Bond of Benj. Hunt to Wm Trego assigned by Trego to Henry Howard.

4 Old 123/May 29-Aug 3 1685/Timothy McNamara and Sarah his wife to Robert Pope: "Buck Valley" near Transquakin Bay, containing 50 a. more or less. Wit: James Pearle, Jacob Jones. James Pearle, atty for Sarah McNamara. Acknowledged Aug 4 1685. Thomas Smithson, Clk.

4 Old 123/Apr 7 1685/John Dyer of the parish of Kingstone in the County of Gloucester in Virginia, planter to Leonard Jones of Somerset County, Maryland, planter: Power of Atty. Proved and produced by Leonard Jones Aug 4 1685 as authority to receive a deed of sale from John Bounds on behalf of Dyer.

4 Old 124/Aug 4 1685/William Brice of Dorchester County, planter and Elinor his wife to Thomas Gillmin of Dorchester County, carpenter: "Brices Range" containing 100 a. more or less, patented to Brice Sep 10 1683. Wit: Henry Howard, Thomas Pattison. Acknowledged Aug 4 1685.

4 Old 125/Jun 2 1685/Richard Holmes of Talbot County and Mary his wife to Joseph Wiggott of the same County, planter: land formerly belonging to the father of Holmes, being part of 1000 a. called "Goodridge Choice" patented to Timothy Goodridge, conveyed by Goodridge to Edward Roe and conveyed by Roe to Nicholas Holmes, late of Talbot County, deceased, father of said Richard Holmes. Two hundred a. on Cabin Creek conveyed. Wit: Richard Willows, Thomas Delahay. Acknowledged Aug 4 1685. Thomas Smithson, Clk.

4 Old 126/Mar 4 1682/Thomas Taylor of Dorchester County, Gent. and Frances his wife to Charles Hutchins of the same County, Gent.: Part of "Taylor's Neglect" on Chiccanoccomocco River. Acknowledeged Jun 5 1683 by Thomas Taylor before Henry Trippe and Edward Pindar. Acknowledged Aug 6 1685 by Frances Taylor. Thomas Smithson, Clk.

4 Old 127/Feb 14 1683/Robert Collier of Somerset County, planter and Elizabeth his wife to John Peirce of Nanticoke in the same County, planter: Land on the NW branch of Nanticoke containing 350 a. more or less, patented to Collier Feb 15 1674, called "Winsor." Wit: William Brereton, James Desheill, Thomas Dashiell, Jeremiah Davis. Acknowledged Feb 15 1683. Thomas Smithson, Clk. Receipt for alienation Mar 6 1683. John Taylor. Sherr.

4 Old 128/Jun 2 1684/John Booth of Dorchester County, carpenter to Joseph Thompson of the same County, planter: "Forrest of Dalamore" on a branch of Chiccanoccomocco River containing 200 a. more or less. Wit: John Hodson, Thomas Hicks. Acknowledged Jun 2 1684. Thomas Smithson, Clk.

4 Old 129/May 22 1683/John Spicer and Thomas Wingod, planters of Dorchester County to William Bourne of the same County, joyner: "Hellens Bumstead" at the head of the eastern branch of Fox Creek which issues out of Hungar River, containing 50 a. Wit: Thomas Pattison, James Pattison. Elizabeth, wife of Thomas Wingod. Acknowledged Jun 6 1683. Thomas Smithson, Clk.

4 Old 130/Aug 5 1685/Stephen Gary of Dorchester County to Gournay Crowe, Gent.: Land on western side of NW branch of Transquakin River, called "Porpeigham," adj land of John Rawlins and containing 300 a. more or less. Wit: Henry Griffin, Thomas Veigch. Acknowledged Aug 6 1685. Thomas Smithson, Clk. Receipt for 12 shillings for alienation, Aug 7 1685. John Taylor, Sherr.

4 Old 130/Feb 23 1683/4/Thomas Taylor of Dorchester County and Ann his wife to Joseph Smith of the same County, planter: Bond to convey 300 a. called

"The Plaines" on the north side of Hunting Creek adj "Hunting Fields," also adj land formerly laid out for Nicholas Painter. Wit: John Braday, William Carr.

4 Old 130/Mar 6 1682/John Brooke of Dorchester County, Chyrurgeon to Christopher Waller of the same place: Bond re conveyance of 200 a. from Brooke to Waller. Wit: Mnthony Dawson, Henry Howard.

4 Old 131/Feb 5 1684/5/Abraham Floyd of the Island of Barbadoes to William Trego of Maryland, mariner: Apprenticeship for the term of eleven years, to learn the art of Navigation. John and Sarah Demew, father and mother of Abraham Floyd. Sarah, wife of William Trego. Wit: Richard Crockford, William Hunter, Charles Spencer.

4 Old 131/Sep 13 1684/Elizabeth Howell, spinster to William Stanley of Gallaway, merchant: Indenture for 4 years from the arrival of the ship "Speedwell" of London, John Inland, Master, in Maryland or Pennsylvania from the prot of Gallaway. Wit: George Yeeden, John Ball, Pattr. Connolly. "Speedwell" of London cast anchor in the capes of Virginia Jan 23 1684. Wit: James Asherrne(?), Dennis Conolly. Mar 7 1684 - Thomas Cooke now master of the within bound Elizabeth Howell. Wit: John Taylor, John Woodward.

4 Old 132/Aug 27 1684/Jennitt Pooton of Gleaston in Lancaster to Thomas Sandiford of Liverpool in Lancaster: Indenture to serve for 4 years in return for pasage to America. Wit: Robert Seacome, Majr., Thomas Sandiford, "towne clerke of the Burrough of Leverpoole." Arrived Jan 9 1684/5.

4 Old 132/Sep 24 1684/John Pottinger to Francis Raules: Indenture to serve 4 years in return for passage to America. Wit: Sr. William Clutterbuck, Kt., J. Mason.

4 Old 132/May 28 1685/William Dolebery and Francis Harbin to Thomas Pattison of Dorchester County: Power of Atty. Wit: Bat. Ennalls, Jno. Harbin. Proved Aug 5 1685.

4 Old 133/May 28 1685/William Dolebery of Dorchester County, Admr. of William Bennett deceased, to Thomas Pattison of Dorchester County: Power of Atty. Wit: Bartho. Ennalls, Jno. Harbin. Proved Aug 5 1685. Thomas Smithson, Clk.

4 Old 133/Sep 1 1685/Daniell Willard of Dorchester County, planter to William Willoughby of the same County, mason: "Yorke" between the head of Little Choptank River and the head of Fishing Creek, containing 50 a. more or less. Wit: Isaac Vicars, Benj. Priestley. Acknowledged Sep 1 1685. Thomas Smithson, Clk. Alienation paid.

4 Old 134/Sep 8 1684/Michaell Wyatt of Dorchester County, planter to William Walker of the same County, planter: Bond re deed dated Jul 24 1682 for 1/2 of "Blinkhornes Poynt" sold by Walker to Wyatt. Wit: John Taylor, Thomas Smithson. Proved Feb 10 1684/5. Thomas Smithson, Clk.

4 Old 134/Jun 18 1685/Honnor Murphey of Dorchester County, spinster, to John Boswell of the same County, planter: Apprenticeship of John Murphey, son of Honnor Murphey, to serve for the period of 18 years from the last day of Sep next after the date hereof. Wit: Benj. Hunt, Robert Boswell.

4 Old 135/Dec 4 1682/Bartholomew Ennalls of Dorchester County, Gent. to Francis Howard of the same County, planter: Part of 500 a. called "Beaver Neck" on Transquakin River, purchased by Ennalls from John Edmondson. Wit: John Foster, William Stephens.

4 Old 135/Aug 5 1685/John Spicer of Dorchester County, planter to Jacob Jones: Land between the two branches of the head of Tedious Creek in Dorchester County, containing 50 a. more or less called "Saffron Walden," patented to Spicer. Wit: Robert Pope, Thomas Smithson. Acknowledged Aug 5 1685. Thomas Smithson, Clk. Alienation paid to Jno. Taylor, Sher.

4 Old 136/Mar 9 1685/John Spicer to John Prout: Bond re sale made by Spicer to Prout. Wit: Hen. Howard, Benj. Priestley. Acknowledged Aug 5 1685. Thomas Smithson, Clk.

4 Old 136/Mar 9 1685/Thomas Wingod and John Spicer to Jno. Prout: Bond re sale made between Wingod and Spicer on the one part and Prout on the other part. (Signed by John Spicer only). Wit: Hen. Howard, Benj. Priestley. Acknowledged Aug 5 1685 by John Spicer. Thomas Smithson, Clk.

4 Old 137/Mar 9 1684/5/Thomas Wingod and John Spicer to John Prout: "Waxford" on the west side of Goose Creek issuing out of Fishing Bay, containing 50 a. more or less. (Signed by John Spicer only.) Wit: Hen. Howard, Benj. Priestley. Acknowledged Aug 5 1685 by John Spicer. Thomas Smithson, Clk.

4 Old 137/Mar 9 1685/John Spicer to John Prout: "Haverill" on the west side of Goose Creek between "Buck Valley," "Waxford," "Steeple Bumstead" and "Doe Park" and containing 50 a. more or less. Also "Steeple Bumstead" containing 50 a. more or less. Wit: Hen. Howard, Benj. Priestley. Acknowledged Aug 5 1685. Thomas Smithson, Clk.

4 Old 139/Aug 5 1685/Thomas Taylor to Anthony Squires and William Carr: "Goodridges Choice," adj land of William Butler and containing 100 a. more or less. Wit: Hen. Howard, Thomas Flowers. Acknowledged Aug 4 1685. Thomas Smithson, Clk.

4 Old 139/May 12 1685/John Bounds of Somerset County, carpenter and Mabel his wife to John Dyer of the Colony of Virginia: "Lempster" containing 300 a. more or less on the NW branch of Nanticoke River. Wit: Samuel Crayker, John Richardson. Leonard Jones of Somerset County, atty for John Dyer. Acknowledged Aug 5 1685. Thomas Smithson, Clk. Alienation paid Aug 4 1685. John Taylor, Sherr.

4 Old 140/Jan 15 1683/4/Thomas Smithson of Miles River in Talbot County to his kinsman Thomas Smithson of Dorchester County, Gent.: Power of Atty. Wit: John Hollins, Saml. Hatton.

4 Old 141/Sep 1685/William Cheesman and Judith hiw wife of Dorchester County to Thomas Colton of the same County: 50 a. called "Cheesmans Gore" on Great Choptank River and on the east side of Hunting Creek, at the mouth of the creek, adj "Bretts Hope" and "Blinkhornes Poynt." Wit: Hen. Howard, Thomas Taylor, Lewis Page. Acknowledged Aug 6 1685. Alienation paid Feb 28 1683/4. John Taylor, Sherr.

4 Old 141/May 1686/William Elliott of England, Gent. To Thomas Smithson of Dorchester County: Release. Ordered to be recorded. Thomas Smithson, Clk., per Benj. Priestley, sub-clk.

4 Old 142/May 30 1685/Timothy McNamara of Dorchester County to John People of the same place: "Batchelors Fancy" on a branch of Blackwater River, containing 50 a. Wit: Francis Anderton, Phine. Blackwood. Acknowledged Aug 5 1685. Thomas Smithson, Clk.

4 Old 142/Oct 6 1683/Thomas Hooker of West River in Maryland to John Edmondson of the same Province: Power of Atty re property in New York. Wit: Thomas Montfort, Wm. Porter. Acknowledged by John Edmondson to be the act and deed of Thomas

Hooker, Jan 6 1685. Thomas Smithson, Clk.

4 Old 143/Sep 2 1685/John Richardson of Dorchester County to Thomas Taylor, planter: 200 a. called "Addition" on the north side of Cabin Creek adj a parcel formerly laid out for Richardson called "Goodridge Choice." Wit: ... Staplefort, Joseph Fisher. Acknowledged by John Edmondson, atty for John Richardson, Sep 2 1685. Thomas Smithson, Clk.

4 Old 143/Aug 6 1685/Christopher Waller of Dorchester County, planter to John Brooke of the same County, Chirurgeon: Bond re deed from Waller to Brooke. Wit: Thos Cooke, Edward Cooke. Acknowledged Sep 1 1685. Thomas Smithson, Clk.

4 Old 145/Oct 1684/Thomas Hooker of Ann Arundell County, planter to Michall Wyman of Talbot County, planter: "Parthomell" on the south side of Great Choptank River some two miles betow the dividing of the river, containing 100 a. more or less. Also "Parthomell" containing 50 a. more or less. Wit: Thomas Skillington, John Dyne. Acknowledged Sep 1 1685 by John Edmondson, atty for Thomas Hooker. Thomas Smithson, Clk. Alienation paid Jan 6 1685/6. William Hill, sub Sherr.

4 Old 146/Sep 1 1685/John Pritchett of Dorchester County, planter to William Warren of the same County, planter: "Little Goshen" near Tedious Creek, adj "Galloway" and containing 50 a. more or less. Wit : Benj. Priestley, Hen. Howard. Margery Pritchett, wife of John Pritchett. Acknowledged Sep 1 1685. Thomas Smithson, Clk.

4 Old 147/Aug 3 1685/Thomas Smithson of Talbot County, Gent. to Benj. Priestley of the same County: "Arcadia" at the head of the branches of Chiccanacomocco, containing 206 a. more or less. Wit: Hen. Howard, Tho. Smithson. Acknowledged Sep 2 1685. Thomas Smithson, Clk. Alienation paid Aug 6 1685. John Taylor, Sherr.

4 Old 148/Aug 6 1685/Christopher Waller of Dorchester County, planter to John Brooke of the same County, Chirurgeon: 200 a. called "Hazelwood" on the west side of the NW branch of Transquakin River. Wit: Thomas Cooke, Edward Cooke. Acknowledged Sep 1 1685. Thomas Smithson, Clk.

4 Old 148/Aug 31 1685/Mary Colton, wife of Thomas Colton to Benj. Priestley: Power of Atty to acknowledge "Cheesemans Gore" to John Wade. Wit: Jno. Richardson, William Walker. Proved mar 2 1685/6 before Barth. Ennalls and Edward Pindar. Thomas Smithson, Clk.

4 Old 149/Oct 13 1685/Patrick Harwood of the "County of Durham in ye province of Maryland, planter, but of late of ye county of Dorchester in ye afsd Province" to John Stevens of Dorchester County, Gent.: "Entrim" containing 100 a. more or less, between Stevens beaver dam branch and Transquakin Road. Wit: Thomas Smithson, Francis Anderton. Acknowledged Oct 13 1685 before Henry Trippe and Edward Pindar. Thomas Smithson, Clk.

4 Old 150/Sep 1 1685/Thomas Colton of Dorchester County, planter to John Wade of the same County, planter: "Cheesmans Gore" at the mouth of Hunting Creek, adj "Bretts Hope" and "Blinkhornes Poynt" and containing 50 a. more or less. Wit: ... Pritchett, Thomas Taylor. Acknowledged by Thomas Colton Sep 1 1685; acknowledged by Mary Colton Sep 5 1685; acknowledged by Benj. Priestley, atty for Mary Colton, Mar 2 1685/6 before Barth. Ennalls and Edward Pindar. Thomas Smithson, Clk. Alienation paid Apr 25 1686. John Taylor, Sherr.

4 Old 151/Nov 16 1685/William Bourn of Dorchester County to Kempton Mabbott of the same County: "Hellens Bumstead" at the head of Fox Creek containing 50

a. more or less. Also "Bournes Meadows" on a creek of Hungar River called
Fox Creek between Hoopers Creek and Tapticoes Creek, adj "Hellens Bumstead"
and containing 50 a. more or less. Also "Buck Ridge" on the north side of
Hoopers Creek, which is a branch of Fox Creek, opposite the land Spicer and
Wingott called "Colchester" and containing 50 a. more or less. Wit: Susanna
Moss, John Bracksley. Acknowledged Jan 5 1685/6. Joseph Stanaway, atty for
Mary Bourn, wife of William Bourn. Alienation paid. John Taylor, Sherr.

4 Old 152/Nov 18 1685/James Peterkin to Richard Adams: "Plain Dealing" on the
side of Transquakin River adj "Partnership" and containing 200 a. Wit: John
Taylor, Benj. Hunt. Acknowledged Nov 18 1685. Thomas Smithson, Clk.

4 Old 153/Nov 13 1685/Edward Taylor of Dorchester County to John McKeell of
the same county: Land on the south side of Little Choptank River and the
western side of Fishing creek, called "Cedar Poynt," containing 50 a. Also
part of "Fishing Creek Poynt" in the occupation of Edward Taylor according to
division made by Thomas Taylor and Daniel Clarke between Edward Taylor and
William Hill. Wit: John Ford, John Mackeel Junr., Benj. Priestley. Acknowledged Nov 18 1685. Elizabeth Taylor, wife of Edward Taylor. Thomas Smithson, Clk. Alienation paid Feb 19 1685/6 ("Fishing Creek Poynt" containing 75
a.). John Taylor, Sherr.

4 Old 154/Nov 13 1685/John Mackeell of Dorchester County to Edward Taylor: Land on the south side
of Little Choptank River on the south side of Fishing Creek and on the western side of a small creek
called Back Creek which issues out of the south side of Fishing Creek; within the bounds of "Garys
Chance" but now known by the name of the "Fifty Acres." Wit: John Ford, John Mackee, Junr., Benj.
Priestley. Acknowledged by John Edmondson to be the act and deed of Thomas Hooker, Jan 6 1685.

4 Old 156/Feb 21 1687/Joseph Stanaway of Dorchester County, Planter to Robert
Robinson of the same County, planter: "Wadles Desire" on Fox Creek which
issues out of Hungar River, containing 50 a. more or less. Wit: David E...,
John Jeferson. Acknowledged Jun 5 1688 by Joseph Stanaway and Elizabeth his
wife, before Thomas Taylor and John Brooks. Sam Smith, Clk.

4 Old 158/Feb 1 1685/6/John Woodward of Dorchester County and Martha his wife
to Joakim Paggett and Thomas Kemball of Boston in New England, Merchants:
"Papaw Thickett" containing 100 a. on the south side of Little Choptank
River, at the head of Fishing Creek and on Teverton Creek, granted to Thomas
Manning, conveyed by Cooke to Thomas Newton, and conveyed by Edward Newton,
son and heir of said Thomas Newton, to John Woodward. Also "Papaw Thickett
Poynt" held by the afsd patent and conveyed in the same way as "Papaw Thick-
ett," containing 50 a. more or less. Also "the Angle" laid out for Edward
Newton and conveyed by him to John Woodward, containing 6 a. more or less.
Also "Woodwards Content" laid out for John Woodward as part of a warrant of
200 a. Wit: Thomas Smithson, Benj. Priestley. Acknowledged Feb 4 1685/6
before Thomas Taylor and Edward Pindar. Thomas Smithson, Clk. Alienation
paid Feb 4 1685/6. John Taylor, Sherr. Margrett Newton, wife of Edward
Newton, under age when Indenture was drawn but now 21 years of age, acknowledged deed Feb 9 1685/6 before Thomas Taylor and Edward Pindar. Thomas
Smithson, Clk. Wit: William Stanley, John Plumer.

4 Old 160/May 1 1684/John Evans and Susannah his wife of Dorchester County to
Edward Pinder of the same County, Gent.: 1/2 of "Goodridges Choyce" adj land
of Andrew Gray, on the north side of Cabin Creek and containing 300 a. more
or less. Acknowledged May 1 1684 before Henry Trippe and Charles Hutchins.

4 Old 161/Feb 2 1680/Edward Newton of Dorchester County, planter to Morrice
Matthews of the same County, planter: 100 a. called "Newtons Desire" on

Little Choptank River and Garys Creek, on the west side of the creek, adj land formerly laid out for Daniel Clark and now in the possession of Newton. Wit: Griff. Jones, Hen. Howard.

4 Old 163/Nov 6 1685/John Davis of Dorchester County, planter to William Walker of the same County, planter: 1/2 of "Poplar Ridge" on the south side of Hogg Island treek, containing 290 a. more or less. Wit: Benj. Priestley, George Prous.

4 Old 165/Jun 4 1686/Thomas Cooke and Ann his wife of Dorchester County to John Foorde of the same County: Part of "Paris" on the west side of Blackwater River. Wit: Benj. Priestley. Acknowledged Jun 3 1686 before Thomas Taylor and Jacob Loockerman.

4 Old 166/Mar 2 1685/Thomas Pattison of Dorchester County, wine cooper to John Foster of the same County, planter: "Exchange" on the northwest side of the northeast branch of the head of Transquakin River, containing 200 a. more or less. Patent first granted to William Willoby and conveyed by him to said Thomas Pattison Oct 7 1674. Wit: Henry Trippe, Edward Pindar. Acknowledged by Ann Pattison, wife of Thomas Pattison.

4 Old 167/John Barnes of Dorchester County, Gent. to Henry Hooper of the same County, Gent.: "Martins Hundred" on the north side of Nanticoke River, near the head of the river, on Herring Creek, containing 1750 a. more or less. Wit: Benj. Priestley, Gournay Crowe. Grace Barnes, wife of John Barnes.

4 Old 168/May 13 1686/Thomas Bushell of Ackamack County, Virginia, to Henry Hooper of Dorchester County: Power of Atty to Collect debts due Bushell from Kempton Mabbott and Charles Powell. Wit: Tim Macknamara, Stephen Selous. Proved by testimony of Timothy Macknamara Mar 5 1686/7. Thomas Cooke, Clk.

4 Old 169/Jun 1 1686/Thomas Taylor of Dorchester County, Gent. and Frances his wife to Edward Williams: "Bristow" on the northwest branch of Transquakin River, containing 300 a. adj land formerly laid out for Henry Osburne. Wit: John Ryan, John Southe, Benj. Priestley.

4 Old 170/May 5 1686/Henry Griffin and Elizabeth his wife to John Taylor: "Griffens Chance" containing 200 a. on the west side of Cone Creek, adj land of John Taylor called "Balea." Wit: Edward Pindar, Gournay Crowe.

4 Old 171/Jun 15 1686/Thomas Smithson of Dorchester County, Gent. to John Taylor of the same county, Gent.: Power of atty to convey "Sector" and "Cambre Lake" sold by Smithson to Thomas Hicks, and to sell a tract of land called "Hellkettles." Wit: Edward Pindar, Benj. Priestley. Proved Sep 7 1686 before Henry Trippe and John Hudson.

4 Old 172/Feb 2 1685/Benj. Hunt of Dorchester County, Gent. to Thomas Smithson of the same County, Gent.: "Ripplin" containing 150 a. on Chicinocomacco River, on the western side of the River, adj "Northwalsum." Wit: William Hill, Benj. Priestley. Acknowledged Feb 3 1685/6.

4 Old 173/Mar 2 1685/Henry Aldred and Mary his wife of Dorchester County to John Woodward of the same County, Gent.: "Bintree" on a branch of Blackwater River, containing 50 a. more or less. Also "Dess" on a branch of Blackwater, containing 17 a. more or less. Also "Aye" on a branch of Blackwater containing 17 a. more or less. Wit: Benj. Priestley, John Foorde. Acknowledged Mar 7 1695/6 before Henry Trippe and Edward Pindar.

4 Old 174/Nov 29 1694/John Edward, Lew. Woodnett, Arthur Whiteley, Jacob Loockerman, Edw. Cooke, Phillip Williams, Wm Dossey, Thos Wall, Benj. Priest-

ley, Thos Veitch and Lewis Page, Creditors of Henry Harman late of Dorchester County, carpenter, deceased, to the widow of said Harman: Release. Wit: John Newton, Christian Arlle.

4 Old 175/Mary 27 1686/John Spicer of Dorchester County to Robert Poope of the same County: "Doe Parke" on the west side of Goose Creek adj "Buck Valley" and containing 50 a. more or less. Wit: Edward Bentall, Andrew Insley.

4 Old 176/Nov 6 1685/William Walker of Dorchester County, planter to George Sprouse of the same County, planter: 1/2 of "Walkers Chance" on Great Choptank River containing 100 a. adj "Goodridges Choyce," the other half of "Walkers Chance" having been sold by Walker to Joseph Wiggott of Talbot County. Wit: Benj. Priestley, John Davis. Alienation paid Jan 1 1685/6. John Taylor, Sherr.

4 Old 178/Oct 29 1682/Joseph Stanaway of Dorchester County to Andrew Insley of the same County: "Stanaways Lott" on the east side of the mouth of Hungar River and on the east side of Fox Creek, containing 90 a. more or less; also "Stanaways Forrest" at the head of the northeast branch of Fox Creek, containing 50 a. more or less. Elizabeth, wife of Joseph Stanaway. Wit: George Fergasson, Hugh Grunfild, Elinor Styth. Acknowledged Nov 28 1683.

4 Old 179/Feb 19 1686/Agreement between William Chesman of Dorchester County and William Walker of the same County, re division of land called "Poplar Ridge." Wit: Alice Goderd, Thomas Compton, John Flaherty. Acknowledged Jun 1 1686.

4 Old 179/Jan 6 1685/Sherry Wansey of Dorchester County, planter, Executor of Joseph Soane of the said County, Chyrurgeon, deceased, to John Edmondson of Talbot County: "Guinney Plantation" containing 100 a. more or less; "Gotham" containing 150 a. more or less; and "Outrange" containing 1000 a. more or less. Wit: Griff Jones, John Stevens, William Eliot.

4 Old 180/Sep 1 1685/Thomas Taylor of Dorchester County, planter to Joseph Smith of the same County, Gent.: "Planes" on the north side of Hunting Creek adj "Hunting Field," also adj land of Nicholas Painter and containing 300 a. more or less. Wit: Abraham Blagge, Richard Owen.

4 Old 181/Mar 15 1676/William Foorde of Dorchester County, Gent. to Thomas Cooke of London, Merchant: "Carlisle" on the west side of Blackwater River, containing 100 a.; also "Browelstone" on the west side of Blackwater River containing 100 a.; also "Paris" on the west side of Blackwater, adj lands of Samuell Milington and James Selby, and containing 416 a. Wit: John Dossey, Edward Cooke. Acknowledged Mar 15 1676 before Henry Trippe and John Brooke.

4 Old 183/Jun 7 1687/John Wade of Dorchester County and Elizabeth his wife to Joseph Wiggott of Talbot County: "Chesmans Gore" formerly in the possession of Thomas Colton and conveyed by him to said John Wade, at the mouth of Hunting Creek adj "Blinhornes Poynt" and containing 50 a. Wit: Nicolls, Dilahay, Carr. Acknowledged Aug 2 1687, before Henry Trippe and John Hodson.

4 Old 185/Aug 22 1687/William Parratt of Talbot County to George Hort: 100 a., the uppermost part of "Brotherly Kindness." Wit: John Teat, William Cooper, Sam Crayker. Acknowledged Sep 7 1687 before Henry Trippe and Jacob Loockerman.

4 Old 185/Sep 6 1687/Gournay Crowe of Dorchester County to John Brooke, Chyrurgion: 100 a. called "Crowes Nest" on the north side of Transquakin River. Wit: Richard Owen, Benjamin Hunt. Acknowledged Sep 8 1687. Sam Smith, Clk.

4 Old 186/Aug 1 1687/Anthony Thompson of Dorchester County to William Jones of the same County: "Thompsons Range" on the north side of the north west branch of Blackwater River on the east side of the mouth of Thompsons Creek, containing 100 a. more or less. Wit: Hen. Howard, Thomas Wall. Acknowledged Sep 7 1687 before Thomas Taylor and John Brooke.

4 Old 187/Mar 28 1686/John Edmondson of Talbot County, Gent. to Thomas Smithson of Dorchester County: "Guinney Plantation" containing 100 a. more or . less; also "Gotham" containing 150 a. more or less. Wit: Thos. Taylor, Edw. Pinder. Acknowledged Sep 7 1687. Sam Smith, Clk.

4 Old 188/Sep 17 1685/John Richardson Senr. of Kent County in Pennsylvania to John Edmondson Senr. of Talbot County, Merchant: All his property in Maryland. Wit: Charles Pickering, Thomas Wilson, James Standfield.

4 Old 189/Aug 31 1683/William Parrott and Sarah his wife of Talbot County to John Youngman of the same County: "Edmondsons Reserve" at the mouth of Phillips Creek on the east side of the northeast branch of Great Choptank River. Wit: Anthony Phillips, Benjamin Parratt. Acknowledged Sep 8 1687 before Henry Trippe and Jacob Loockerman.

4 Old 189/Sep 6 1687/Gournay Crowe to John Brooke: land purchased from Stephen Gary late of this County deceased, on the western side of the northwest branch of Transquakin River, called "Porpeigham" containing 300 a. more or less. Wit: Richard Owen, Benj. Hunt. Acknowledged Sep 8 1687. Sam Smith, Clk.

4 Old 190/Oct 12 1687/William Willowby of Dorchester County, planter to Samuel Smith of the said County, Gent.: "Buttwells Choice" at the head of Little Choptank River adj land of Robert Winsmore and containing 100 a. more or less; also "William & Hannahs Choice" on the south side of Little Choptank River, adj "Buttwells Choice" and containing 100 a. more or less. Wit: Gournay Crowe, Hen. Howard. Hannah Willowby, wife of William Willowby.

4 Old 191/Sep 4 1687/William Parratt of Talbot County to Richard Thompson: 200 a. in the freshes of Great Choptank River, part of 1050 a. called "Edmondsons Reserve." Wit: Hen. Howard, Thomas Flowers. Acknowledged Sep 7 1687 before Henry Trippe and Jacob Loockerman.

4 Old 192/Jun 18 1687/Thomas Wall of Dorchester County to Thomas Gordon, Professor of Divinity in the said county: Moyety or 1/2 of "Worgans Chance" formerly pruchased from Thomas Taylor by Edward Sauvage, containing 25 a.; also land on Fishing treek containing 50 a.; also the other moyety of Worgans Chance" containing 50 a.; also "Worgans Adventure" containing 50 a. Wit: Gournay Crowe, Arthur Whiteley. Tracts purchased by Wall from John Edmondson of Talbot County. Acknowledged Aug 2 1687 before Hen. Trippe and Hen. Hooper.

4 Old 193/Aug 2 1687/Kempton Mabbott of Talbot County, Innholder to John Prout of Dorchester County: "Hellens Bumstead" at the head of the eastern branch of Fox Creek which issues out of Hungar River containing 50 a. more or less; also "Bounres Meadowes" on Fox Creek between Hoopers Creek and Tapticoes Creek, containing 50 a. more or less; also "Buckridge" on the north side of Hoopers Creek which is a branch of Fox Creek, adj "Helens Bumstead" and containing 50 a. more or less. Wit: Edward Pinder, Hen. Howard. Acknowledged by Susanna, wife of Kempton (Kym) Mabbott, August 2 1687 before Hen. Trippe and John Woodward.

4 Old 195/1687/John Steward of Dorchester County to Trustrum Mago and
Benjamin Granger, sons of Margaret Granger the wife of Benjamin Granger of
Dorchester County: 1/2 or Moyety of grantor's dwelling plantation, now called
"Pine Swamp," containing 100 a. on the North side of Little Choptank River
near the mouth of the river, but patented by the name of "Talbat County."
Life estate reserved by grantor. Trustrum Mago and Benjamin Granger under 21
years of age at the signing of this deed. Wit: Haselwood, Powell.

4 Old 196/Nov 2 1687/Michaell Wyman of Dorchester County to William Buckly:
"Parthomall," adj land of John Briggs called "Barthomall" and containing 50
a. more or less. Wit: Hen. Howard, Wm Hill. Margarett Wyman, wife of
Michaell Wyman. Acknowledged Nov 1687. Sam Smith, Clk.

4 Old 197/Sep 5 1687/John Edmondson of Talbot County to William Heather of
Dorchester County: 1/2 or Moyety of a tract on Hunting Creek called "Pitts
Hope" containing in the whole 600 a. more or less. Wit: Hen. Howard, Robert
Penewell. Acknowledged Sep 7 1687 before Thos Taylor and John Brooke.

4 Old 198/Jan 10 1686/John Edmondson of Talbot County to John Nicholls of
Dorchester County, planter: 266 a. being half of a tract of 532 a. laid out
for John Richardson called "Richardsons Choice" at the upper end of land
called "Fox Hill" and near Marsh Creek. Wit: John Payne, Thomas Sharp. Sarah,
wife of John Edmondson. Acknowledged Sep 7 1687 before Hen. Trippe and Jacob
Loockerman.

4 Old 199/Oct 15 1686/William Parratt of Talbot County to John Sharp of Dor-
chester County: 250 a. called "Edmondsons Reserve" on Phillips Creek. Wit:
John Brooke, Thomas Taylor. Acknowledged Sep 7 1687 before Hen. Trippe and
Jacob Loockerman.

4 Old 200/Mar 1 1680/Nicholas Mace of Dorchester County, planter to Edward
Taylor of the same County, planter: land in Fishing creek formerly bought
from Peter Sharpe. Wit: Benj. Hunt, Wm Smithson. Acknowledged in open Court.
Wm Smithson, Clk.

4 Old 201/Jan 17 1687/88/William Dorrington of Dorchester County, Gent. to
John Edmondson and William Sharpe of Talbot County and John Stephens of Dorchester County, Gent.: In consideration of the love and affection of Dorrington for his two children William Dorrington and Ann Dorrington, the issue of
his deceased wife Elizabeth Dorrington, alias Winsloe, and for his brother in
law William Winsloe of Dorchester County, he conveys to grantees, in trust,
"Busby" containing 500 a.; "Temple Street" containing 250 a.; "Bowling Green"
containing 19 a.; "Hoggshole" containing 100 a.; "Clift" containing 200 a.;
and "Clifton" containing 200 a., for the benefit of grantor and his children
and brother in law for their lifetimes with remaider, if life tenants leave
no issue, to the Quakers. If Ann Dorrington reaches the age of marriage
during the lifetime of her brother William Dorrington, she is to receive 1/2
interest in 1000 a. at Blackwater belonging to grantor and William Winsloe;
if she dies before reaching the age of marriage, the entire 1000 a. to belong
to Winsloe. Sarah Dorrington, alias Fisher, mentioned as daughter of grantor.
Wit: Hen. Howard, Ann Glassington, Daniel Smith, John Mallington, Arthur
Whitely, Maurice Matthews. Acknowledged Feb 8 1687 in open Court. Sam Smith,
Clk.

4 Old 204/Feb 8 1687/Jeremiah Davis to Thomas Hicks: "Camber Lake" on a branch
of Chickanocomico River, adj "Secter" and containing 100 a. more or less;
also 1/2 Moyety of "Secter," containing 388 a. more or less. Wit: Benj.
Hunt, Andrew Parker. Signed by John Mackeele. Acknowledged by John Mackeele
Feb 8 1687. Sam Smith, Clk.

4 Old 205/Nov 15 1687/William Dolbury of Poole in the county of Dorset, Mariner, to Thomas Athow of Dorchester County, Gent.: Power of Atty. Wit: Thomas Hide, David Dito, Richard Bennett. Proved by Thomas Hide, one of the witnesses, Feb 8 1687.

4 Old 206/Jan 25 1687/Daniel Jones of Kent County in Pennsylvania, planter, to Arthur Whitely of Dorchester County, Innholder: the upper 1/2 of "Harwoods Choice," containing 300 a. on Fishing Creek and Little Choptank River, adj land formerly laid out for Stephen Gary. Wit: John Barnes, Jesper Jessupp. Acknowledged Mar 8 1687 before Thos Taylor and Henry Trippe. Daniel Clarke, atty for Daniel Jones. Power of Atty witnessed by Jesper Jessupp and Katherine Fielding, dated Nov 30 1687 and proved Jan 12 1687 before John Brooke and John Harwood.

4 Old 209/Nov 2 1687/Agreement of Maurice Matthews re use of Matthews' land called "Daniels Pasture" by Thomas Palmer. Acknowledged in open Court Nov 3 1687. Sam Smith, Clk.

4 Old 209/Oct 3 1687/Daniel Clark and Katherine Clark his wife to Katherine Fielding the wife of James Fielding: Mare and colt. Wit: William Saunders, Jane Hubard.

4 Old 209/Apr 25 1688/Thomas Smithson of Dorchester County, Gent. to Bartholomew Ennalls of the same County, Gent.: "Kipling" on the west side of Chickanocomoco River, adj "Northwalsam" and containing 150 a. more or less. Acknowledged in open Court May 1 1688. Sam Smith, Clk.

4 Old 211/May 2 1688/Joseph Smith of Dorchester County, planter to John Alford of the same County, Gent.: 35 a. of land on Hunting Creek and Great Choptank River. "This Deed was tendered by Joseph Smith to Mr. John Alford, in psuance of an Award; in open Court, May the second 1688, Sam Smith, Clk."

4 Old 212/May 2 1688/Joseph Smith of Dorchester County to Thomas Norwine of the same County: 1/2 of "the Plaines" containing by estimation 300 a., on Hunting Creek. Wit: Anthony Squires. Acknowledged in open Court May 2 1688. Sam Smith, Clk.

4 Old 213/Joseph Smith of Dorchester County to Anthony Squires of the same County: 1/2 of 300 a. called "the Plaines" on Hunting Creek adj land of Nicholas Panther. Wit: Hen. Howard, Thos Norwine. Acknowledged in open Court May 2 1688. Sam Smith, Clk.

4 Old 214/Apr 25 1688/Thomas Wall of Dorchester County to Thomas Scott of the same County: land formerly in the tenure of George Martine deceased, on Fishing Creek, called "the Grove" and containing by estimation 150 a. Acknowledged in open Court May 2 1688. Sam Smith, Clk.

4 Old 215/May 1 1688/Thomas Pattison of James Island, wine cooper to Jacob Loockerman of the same nounty, Chirurgeon: "Rochester" at the head of Blinckornes Creek, adj land of Brett Dalender and "Blinckornes Point," also adj "Goodritches Choice" and containing 400 a. more or less. Wit: John Alford, Hen. Howard. Ann Pattison, wife of Thomas Pattison. Acknowledged in open Court May 1 1688. Sam Smith, Clk.

4 Old 216/Dec 6 1687/Thomas Gordon of Dorchester County, professor of Divinity to Thos. Wall of the same County, planter: 1/2 of a parcel of land purchased by Edward Sauvage, deceased, from Thomas Taylor, called "Worgans Chance," containing 25 a. more or less. Also 50 a. on the south side of Fishing Creek. Also the other moyety of "Worgans Chance" containing 50 a.

Also "Worgans Adventure" containing containing 50 a. on the east side of
Fishing Creek, adj land of Robert Harwood, also adj land formerly laid out
for Worgan called "Worgans Creek." Wit: Sam Smith, Hen. Howard. Acknowledged Dec 6 1687 by Henry Howard, atty for Thomas Gordon, before Thomas
Taylor and Henry Trippe.

4 Old 218/May 17 1686/Margaret Harris of Dorchester County, widow, to her son
John Harris: Livestock to be delivered to John Harris when he shall arrive at
age seventeen. Wit: Ellis Thomas, John Richardson. Symon Richardson, atty
for Margaret Harris.

4 Old 219/Oct 28 1684/Joseph Stanaway to Thomas Wingod and John Spicer:
"Southampton" at the mouth of Hungar River and on Fox Creek, containing 100
a. more or less. Also "Fox Point" on the east side of Hungar River and the
east side of Fox Creek, adj "Southampton" and containing 10 a. more or less.
Elizabeth Stanaway, wife of Joseph Stanaway. Wit: Geo. Fergusson, Nathaniel
Saunderson, William Goodin. Acknowledged Jun 5 1688 before Thomas Taylor and
John Brooke. Sam Smith, Clk.

4 Old 220/Dec 12 1688/William Watson of Dorchester County to William Norcome:
Land laid out for Watson at the head of Marshy Creek adj "Contention" and
containing 317 a. more or less. Wit: Robert Winsmore, Phill Pitt. Acknowledged Dec 12 1688 before Thomas Taylor and Jno. Woodward. Thos Pattison,
Clk.

4 Old 221/Mar 4 1688/Thomas Jeanes of Dorchester County, planter to Thomas
Thacker of the same County, planter: Part of "Goulden Quarter" on Chikenaco-
moco River, adj land of Anguish Murrow. Acknowledged Mar 5 1688/9 before
Henry Trippe and John Brooke. Thos. Pattison, Clk.

4 Old 222/Jan 14 1688/Thomas Jeanes to Anguish Morrow of Dorchester County,
planter: part of "Goulden Quarter" on Chikenacomoco River. Acknowledged Mar
5 1688/9 before Henry Trippe and John Brooke. Thos Pattison, Clk.

4 Old 223/Feb 13 1688/William Willoughby and Hanah his wife to Thomas Taylor:
"Bridg North" on Little Choptank River and Hudsons Creek containing 50 a.
more or less. Acknowledged Mar 5 1688/9 before Henry Trippe and John Brooke.
Thos. Pattison, Clk.

4 Old 224/mar 5 1688/William Woodgate of Dorchester County, planter to John
Smith of the same County, cooper: "Leyster" near the head of Nanticoke River
and near a fresh water run called Clear Brook, containing 300 a. more or
less. Acknowledged Mar 5 1688/9 before Henry Trippe and John Brooke. Thos.
Pattison, Clk.

4 Old 225/Jul 19 1688/Anguish Murrow of Dorchester County, planter to Patrick
Rush of the same County, cooper: "Morrow Land" on a branch of Chickencomoco
River, adj "Sector" and containing 100 a. more or less. Wit: John Franke, Wm
Harrisson. Acknowledged Aug 20 1688 before Thos Taylor and John Hodson.
Thos. Pattison, Clk.

4 Old 226/Sep 4 1688/Thomas Taylor and Frances his wife to Daniel Cocks of
Somerset County: "Birdge Neck" on the east side of Chickenacomoco River,
containing 300 a. more or less. Wit: Edward Pindar, Benj. Hunt. Acknowledged Sep 4 1688 before Henry Trippe and Jno. Woodward. Thos Pattison, Clk.

4 Old 227/Dec 2 1687/Henry Howard of Dorchester County to Edward Pindar,
Gent.: "Strawberry Garden" on the NW branch of Transquakin River on the west
side of the river, adj Michaell Masons land and containing 150 a. Wit: Thos.
Smithson, Wm Hill. Acknowledged Mar 7 1687/8 before Thos. Taylor and Jno.
Woodward. Thos. Pattison, Clk.

4 Old 228/Aug 1688/Edward Pindar of Dorchester County, Gent. to Phillip Pitt: "Strawberry Garden" on the NW branch of Transquakin River, on the west side of the river, adj Michaell Masons land and containing 150 a. more or less. Acknowledged in open Court Aug 8 1688. Thomas Pattison, Clk.

4 Old 229/Mar 1 1682/Richard Webster of Sheffield, England, knife cutler, oldest brother and heir of John Webster late deceased, to William Sharpe: Power of Atty re "Edmondsons Desire" containing 1000 a. more or less. Wit: Michaell Newbould, Joseph Hutcheson, Richard Hind. Deposition of Michael Newbold of Sheffield Park Gate in the County of York, Yoeman, aged 58 years or thereabouts, re execution of this deed. Deposition witnessed by Sir John Frederick Knight, formerly Lord Mayor and now one of the Aldermen and Chief Magistrates of the City of London. Sworn before Nicholas Hayward, Notary Public.

4 Old 230/Apr 2 1685/William Sharpe of Talbot County, Atty for Richard Webster of Sheffield, England, heir of John Webster, deceased, to Wm Dare of Cecil County: "Edmondsons Desire" on Edmondsons Creek in Dorchester County, containing 1000 a. Wit: Samuel Abitt, Thomas Abitt, Edward Cafie, William Hallett. Acknowledged Nov 22 1687 before Henry Trippe and Jacob Loockerman. Thomas Pattison, Clk.

4 Old 232/Nov 2 1687/William Dare of Cecil County, planter to John Atkey of Calvert County, merchant: "Edmondsons Desire." Wit: Bart. Ennalls, Jacob Loockerman, Nath. Dare, James Mosley. Acknowledged Nov 2 1687 before Bart. Ennalls and Jacob Loockerman. Thos. Pattison, Clk.

4 Old 233/May 7 1689/Henry Hooper and Mary his wife to John Prowt of the same County, cooper: "Buck Ridge" on Hungar River, Fox Creek and Hoopers Creek, containing 100 a. more or less. Wit: Thos. Pattison, Wm Hill. Acknowledged May 7 1689 in open Court. Thos. Pattison, Clk. Alienation paid May 7 1689. Wm Hill, Sub Sheriff.

4 Old 234/May 8 1689/William Poope of Stratton, England, merchant to Thomas Wall Sr. of Blackwater in Dorchester County: Release of a Judgment confessed by said Wall to Mr. Harbyn and Mr. Dolebury. Wit: Wm Douse, John Haslewood.

4 Old 235/Mar 10 1688/9/William Douse of England, merchant to Thomas Wall Sr. of Dorchester County: Release from a Judgment confessed by said Wall to Mr. Francis Harbins and Mr. William Dolebury. Wit: Richard Forty.

4 Old 235/May 6 1689/William Man of Rappahanock County, Virginia to Benjamin Hunt of Dorchester County: Power of Atty to receive debts due to Mrs. Elizabeth Wilks or her son Rawleigh Traves. Acknowledged May 7 1689. Thos. Pattison, Clk.

4 Old 235/Jun 4 1689/John Prowt of Dorchester County, cooper to John Bramble of the same place, planter: "Prowts Medow" on the west side of the great sound of Transquakin, containing 150 a. more or less. Also 16 a. more or less, being part of "Apes Hill" formerly purchased by Prowt from John Pritchett. Wit: Thos Pattison, Tim McNamara, Robert Pope. Acknowledged in open Court Jun 4 1689. Katherine Prowt, wife of John Prowt. Thos. Pattison, Clk.

4 Old 237/May 7 1689/Thomas Taylor of Dorchester County and Frances his wife to John Hodson of the same County: Land formerly called "Maiden Forrest" on a branch of Chickanacomoco River, containing 100 a. more or less. Wit: Phill Pitt, Benj. Hunt. Acknowledged May 7 1689 in open Court. Thomas Pattison, Clk. Alienation paid May 7 1689. Edward Pindar, Sheriff.

4Old 238/Apr 7 1689/Thomas Ennalls, Mary Ennalls and William Ennalls, Executors of the Last Will and Testament of Bartholomew Ennalls deceased, to

Edward White: 100 a. in Transquakin River, called "Taylors Purchase;" also a tract at the mouth of Blackwater River and near the mouth of Transquakin River, called "Beckwiths Island," being part of "Midleton Grange." Wit: John Elet, Robert Pope. Acknowledged May 7 1689 by Thomas Ennalls for himself, his mother Mary and brother William. Thomas Pattison, Clk.

4 Old 239/war 3 1688/Henry Hooper of Dorchester County, Gent. to Arthur Hart of the same County, planter: "Hogg Quarter" on Transquakin Creek, containing 100 a. more or less. Wit: Thomas Athow, Robert Pope, John Proutt. Acknowledged May 7 1689 in open Court. Thomas Pattison, Clk. Mary, wife of Henry Hooper.

4 Old 241/Apr 20 1689/William Bradly of Dorchester County to Daniel Seares of the same County: "Sewells Choyce" in Transquakin River, containing 100 a. Wit: James Peterkin, John Miller. Acknowledged May 7 1689 before Henry Trippe and Charles Huchens. Thomas Pattison, Clk.

4 Old 242/May 13 1689/John Booth of Dorchester County to Humphrey Molde of the said County: "Ould Bayly" on the north side of Chickenacomoco River containing 100 a. more or less. Wit: Obadiah King, Edward Newton. Acknowledged Jun 4 1689 before Henry Hooper and Jno. Woodward. Thomas Pattison, Clk.

4 Old 243/May 8 1689/Samuell Bramble of Dorchester County to John Draper of the same County: "Middle Land" on Prestons Creek, adj land of Richard Preston and containing 100 a. more or less. Wit: Benj. Hunt, Edward Dawson. Acknowledged Jun 4 1689 in open Court. Thomas Pattison, Clk.

4 Old 244/Jun 5 1689/Andrew Insley of Dorchester County to Edward Bentall: "Coliers Forrest" on the east side of Hungar River containing 50 a. more or less. Wit: Tim McNamara, John Spicer. Acknowledged by Andrew Insley and Elizabeth his wife, Jun 4 1689. Thomas Pattison, Clk.

4 Old 245/Dec 12 1680/Richard Denor Sr of Ann Arundel County, planter to i William Warner of Dorchester County, planter: "Denors Choyce" patented to Denor Jul 2 1668, containing 300 a. more or less. Wit: Thomas Tench, Thomas Driffield, Zach. Allein, Abraham Clarke. Acknowledged in open Court Jun 4 1689. Thomas Pattison, Clk.

4 Old 248/Aug 6 1689/William Jones of Dorchester County, planter to Anthony Thompson of the same County: 1/2 of "Thompsons Range" on a branch of Blackwater River, containing 50 a. more or less. Wit: Thos Skiner, John People. Acknowledged Aug 6 1689 before John Woodward and Henry Hooper. Thomas Pattison, Clk.

4 Old 249/Aug 6 1689/Thomas Hackett and Elizabeth his wife to Jeremiah Hooke: "St. Johns" on the east side of the northwest branch of Nanticoke containing 100 a. more or less. Wit: John Phillips, William Hill. Acknowledged in open Court Aug 6 1689. Thomas Pattison, Clk.

4 Old 249-136/Dec 3 1691/Last Will and Testament of John Hayward: To his eldest son Henry Hayward, "Merchants Adventure" on which Testator now lives; also Testators part of "Beavour Neck," the other part belonging to testator's brother Brancis Hayward. To his second son John Hayward, 64 a. called "Haywards Choice." To his son Francis Hayward, 45 a. called "Haywards Neglect." To testator's three sons, personalty when they come of age. To testator's daughter Mary Hayward, personalty. Testator's wife, not named, Executrix. Wit: Thomas Ennalls, John Bradley. Proved in open Court, Mar 1 1691/2. Hugh Eccleston, Clk.

4 Old 249-1/Jun 3 1690/John Booth to William Carter: "Chesterfield" on Chickenacomoco River, adj "Taylors Neglect" formerly laid out for Thomas Taylor,
and containing 290 a. more or less. Wit: Thomas Pattison. Acknowledged Jun
3 1690 before John Brooke and Jacob Loockerman. Thomas Pattison, Clk.

4 Old 249-2/Jan 1 1689/90/Robert Thornewell to Samuel Bramble: 50 a. called
"Robin Hood Well." Acknowledged Jun 4 1690 by Robert Thornewell and Elizabeth his wife, before Henry Trippe and John ... Thos. Pattison, Clk.

4 Old 249-3/Mar 1 1689/90/Thomas Wall of Dorchester County to John Crimeene
and William Walker of the same County: land purchased from John Newton,
called "Westminster," between the branches of Chicanocomoco River and Transquakin, containing 100 a. more or less. Wit: Gour. Crowe, Phill Pitt. ∴
Acknowledged Jun 3 1690 before John Brooke and Jacob Loockerman. Thos.
Pattison, Clk.

INDEX

References are to Liber and Folio in the original records, as shown at
upper left of each abstract.

AARON Ambrose 2-26. 67. 88
ABABCO (Abaco) Indians 2-115, 116,
138
ABBOTT John 2-133; Samuel 3-213;
Thomas 2-120; William 2-120
ABITT Samuel 4-230; Thomas 4-230
ABRAHAMS (See Abram, Abrams) Isaac
1-33
ABRAM Elizabeth 1-33; Isaac 1-9, 33
ABRAMS Isaac 3-4, 25, 111
ADAMS Abigale 4-72; Richard 1-137,
167; 2-106; 4-152
ADDITION 3-28, 258; 4-143
ADDITION TO BATH 2-79
ADDITION TO CLARKES NECK 4-105
ADVENTURE 3-213
AGG (See Ogg) James 3-44, 192, 254;
4-31, 43
AHEARNE Phillip 4-86
ALDRED Henry 1-83; 3-31; 4-51, 53,
173; Mary 4-51, 53, 173
ALDREDGE Henry 1-55
ALEXANDER Thomas 3-120
ALEXANDER'S PLACE 1-148; 2-30, 32,
39, 91, 109, 109; 4-101
ALFORD Edward 2-29, 90, 130;
Elizabeth 3-199; Hannah 2-109, 149;
John 1-68; 3-43, 172, 175, 177, 186,
199; 4-78, 111, 112, 211, 215;
Joseph 2-4, 100, 106, 109, 136; Mary
2-29
ALL THREE OF US 3-100
ALLDERSON Thomas 2-144
ALLEIN Zach 4-245
ALLEN Francis 2-118, 143; Mary 2-143
ALLENDER - SeeDalender
ALOMBY George 4-55
ANCHOR AND HOPE 3-91, 133, 209
ANDERSON John 2-147
ANDERSON'S NECK 2-147
ANDERSON'S NECK REGULATED 2-147
ANDERTON Francis 1-125, 130; 2-79,
162; 4-68, 142, 149; James 2-137
ANDERTON'S POINT 2-113
ANDREWS Marcus 2-148
ANDREWS CHANCE 3-103, 225
ANDREWS COVE 4-33
ANDREWS FORTUNE 2-163
ANDREWS MARSH 3-268; 4-23
ANDREWS POINT 3-225
ANGLE 4-158
ANNEMESICK (Annamesex) 1-15, 17

APES HILL 3-138, 156, 158; 4-235
APPLEBY 3-222
ARCADIA 1-196; 4-147
ARLLE Christian 4-174
ARMITAGE HUNDRED 2-102
ARMSTRONG Frances 1-44, 46; Francis
1-46, 50, 52, 88, 131; 3-1, 33
ARMSTRONG'S BAY 1-50, 52; 3-183
ARMSTRONG'S FOLLY 1-22, 31, 71, 131;
3-17, 109
ARMSTRONG'S HOGG PENN 1-44
ARMSTRONG'S QUARTER 1-192, 193; 2-9
ARNOLD Richard 3-2
ASHBOURN 3-4, 25
ASHBY Edward 1-56
ASHERRNE James 4-131
ASHLEY Thomas 3-37, 224, 235
ATHOW Thomas 4-205, 239
ATKEY John 4=232
ATKINS John 4-121
ATTKINS John 1-187
ATTOWATTOCOQUM (Attowattocoquin) 2-22,
55, 56
AVERY Anne - See Anne Daldson: John
1-29, 31; 2097; 3-124
AYE 2-151; 4-173

BACK CREEK 1-33; 3-21, 111; 4-154
BAKER John 2-113; 4-84
BALEA 4-170
BALL John 4-131
BALLFOUR Will 4-114
BANKES Thomas 4-44
BARBADOES 4-95
BARBER John 1-74
BSRDON Charles 3-2
BARNES Grace 4-70, 167; John 4-70,
84, 167, 206
BARRATT Mary 2-79
BARREN CREEK 4-103
BARRICRAFT Edward 2-95; Mary 2-95
BARRINGTON William 1-87
BARRON POINT 2-100
BARTHOMALL 4-196
BASEY Joanna 3-25; Michaell 2-25, 83
BATCHELDORS HOPE 2-87
BATCHELORS FANCY 4-142
BATCHELORS FOLLY 2-127
BATCHELORS LOSS 2-49
BATEMAN Jonathan 3-148
BATES John 4-50

-79-

BRANNOCK Ann 2-148; Edmond 1-18, 54,
83; 3-78, 222; John 1-160, 161; 2-133;
John Jr 2-133; Margaret 2-133; Rachell
2-148; Thomas 2-61, 96, 133, 148;
Thomas Jr 2-133
BRANNOCK'S ADVENTURE 1-54
BRANCOK - See Brannock
BREDA 3-95
BRERETON William 4-127
BRETT William 3-17, 18, 24, 26, 109
BRETT'S HOPE 3-22, 213; 4-19, 88, 141,
150
BRICE Elinor 4-124; William 1-8, 139;
3-85, 118, 169, 198; 4-57, 124
BRICES RANGE 4-124
BRIDGE NECK 4-226
BRIDGE NORTH 4-48, 223
BRIGGS John 1-143, 174; 3-15; 4-196
BRILLON Thomas 2-70
BRISTOW 4-169
BRITT - See Brett
BRITT'S HOPE 2-124
BROAD MARSH 1-86, 88
BROKEN WHARFE 4-107
BROOK John - See John Brookes
BROOKES (Brooke) Henry 3-25;
John 1-29, 55, 104, 121, 122,
126, 127, 129, 147, 148, 155, 167,
181; 2-154; 3-4, 25, 34, 45, 65, 86,
105, 125, 129, 135, 138, 148, 151,
162, 164, 169, 181, 182, 183, 189,
190, 192, 198, 207, 242, 262, 4-14,
17, 18, 30, 32, 49, 51, 66, 68, 70,
71, 72, 74, 87, 93, 98, 101, 103, 121,
130, 143, 148, 156, 181, 185, 186,
189, 197, 199, 206, 219, 221, 222,
223, 224, 249-1, 249-3; Katherine
3-189, 190; Michael 1-161
BROOKES OUTHOLD 3-181
BROOKS Michaell 3-189
BROTHERLY KINDNESS 2-110; 4-185
BROUGH Joseph 3-203
BROUGHAN Patrick 2-40, 170
BROUGHTON - See Wroughton
BORWELL STONE 3-91; 4-181
BROWN Charles 2-37, 42; Elizabeth
3-189; James 3-40, 122; Naomi 2-9;
Thomas 1-71; 2-9; 3-51, 189; William
1-172, 173
BROWNE - See Brown
BROXOME Thomas 3-36, 212
BRUFF Richard 2-121; Thomas 2-118
BRUKSHER James 2-167

BUCKLAND 1-137
BUCKLEY William 1-143; 4-196
BUCK RIDGE 4-151, 193, 233
BUCK VALLEY 3-265; 4-123, 137, 175
BULL POINT 2-77, 155
BULL POYNT 4-95
BULLEN John 2-61
BUNDELIN John Rudolphus 2-127
BUNNELL Fields 2-82
BURKE Thomas 2-42
BURN William 2-63
BUSBY 1-106; 2-62, 115; 3-205; 4-29,
201
BUSHELL Thomas 4-168
BUTLER James 3-213; William 1-183,
184
BUTTLER William 3-118; 4-139
BUTTE James 2-94
BUTTON John 3-117; 4-80, 96, 101;
Mary 4-80
BUTTWELL Richard 1-8, 71
BUTTWELL'S CHOICE 1-8; 3-169; 4-36,
51, 190
BUTWELL Richard 3-218; 4-18

CABIN BRANCH 3-135
DABIN CREEK 1-108, 139, 140, 156,
158, 182, 183, 184; 2-16, 27, 44, 53,
87, 104, 113; 3-28, 47, 50, 79, 81,
85, 118, 167, 205, 257; 4-114, 117,
125, 143, 160
CADMORE Richard 3-268
CAFIE Edward 4-230
CALLIE 1-110
CALVERT Charles 1-68, 74; Jane
(Sewell) 2-53; Philip 2-153; 4-5, 22
CAMBRE LAKE 4-68, 171, 204
CAMBRIDGE 1-148; 2-2, 21, 23, 69, 86,
118
CAMBRIDGE ADDITION 2-2
CAMPBELL Walter 1-155; 2-3, 26;
Walter (Justice) 2-14, 18, 19, 21,
22, 25, 40
CANNER Thomas 2-38, 39
CANNING William 3-3
CANNON James 2-99, 171; Thomas 2-99
CANON - See Canning
CANTERBURY 2-96; 3-173
CAPPS John 4-65, 103
CARLYLE 3-91, 210; 4-181
CARNEY Robert 1-145
CARR William 4-66, 130, 139
CARTER William 4-249-1

Thomas 1-108, 110, 130, 148, 153, 160, 161; 3-201; 4-7, 9, 71, 76, 131, 143, 148, 158, 165, 168, 181
COOK'S POINT 2-140
COOLEY George 3-45, 74, 75, 168, 183
COOPER Richard 2-121; William 4-185
COPPEN Ann 3-144
COQUERICUS FIELDS 4-97
CORNELISU John 4-3
CORNISH Richard 3-167
COTTERELL John 2-66, 67, 88; Lucretia 2-66, 67, 88
COTTLE Katherine 3-91
COTTMAN Joseph 2-118
COUGHLAN John 3-183
COULTON - See Colton
COURSEY William 1-167; 3-33
COVINGTON Abraham 2-171
COWLEY - See Cooley
CRATCHER Samuel 2-101
CRAWFORD James 3-186
CRAYKER Samuel 4-139, 185
CRICK 4-72
CRICKHILS Samuell 1-44
CRIMEENE John 4-249-3
CROCKETT John 2-45
CROCKFORD Richard 4-131
CROFT Thomas 3-240, 254
CRONEEN Daniel 2-130
CRONEY Daniel 2-90
CROSS James 3-227, 229, 249; William 3-167

CROSSES James 1-178
CROWE Gournay(Gourney) 1-116, 171; 3-20, 60, 66, 71, 86, 98, 100, 107, 111, 117; 4-1/2, 16, 21, 23, 36, 44, 58, 110, 113, 119, 130, 167, 170, 185, 189, 190, 192, 249-3
CROWES NEST 4-185
CUDMAN Richard 3-231
CULLEN John 2-96, 134; Sarah 2-129; William 2-129
CULLINGBURROW Thomas 2-144
CUMBERLAND 2-164
CUPER Simon 1-146
CURTICE Elizabeth 4-10; John 3-97, 168; 4-10
CURTIS (See also Curtice) Thomas 2-93
CURWEN George 4-84

DADWINS CREEK 2-99
DALAMORE - See Forrest of Dalamore
DALDSON Anne 3-124
DALENDER Brett 3-97, 213; 4-10, 19, 61, 215

DALES COVE 3-169, 180
DALLANY Anthony 3-182
DALLENDER - See Dalender
DANIELL Thomas 3-144, 148; 4-103
DANIELL'S PASTURE 3-41, 43; 4-209
DARBY 2-156
DARBY John 3-30, 54
DARDAN Stephen 3-81
DARE Nath. 4-232; William 4-230, 232
DASHIELL James 4-127; Thomas 4-127
DAVICE (See also Davis) Henry 4-99
DAVIS (See Davice) Abigale 4-72; : Elizabeth 2-49; Henry 2-7, 49, 165, 174; Hopkins 3-177; humphrey 3-97; Jeremiah 4-68, 127, 204; John 1-113, 2-18, 21, 77, 132, 137, 145, 153, 159, 165, 172; 4-10, 66, 106, 163, 176; Margaret 2-165; Precilla 4-17; Susanna 4-106; T. 2-13; Thomas 2-165
DAVIS CREEK 4-111
DAWSON Anthony 1-35, 89, 94, 148, 169, 176; 3-34, 86, 127, 137, 183, 208, 209, 210; 4-93, 101, 121, 130; Edward 4-243; James 2-111; John 2-13; Rebecca 1-148; 3-183; Richard 3-90
DAWSONS CHANCE 3-183
DEAN Michael 2-8, 29
DEANE - See Dean
DEEN - See Dean
DEHINOYOSSA Johannas 2-50
DELAHAY ... 4-66; Thomas 4-125
DELLANDER - See Dalender
DEMEW John 4-131; Sarah 4-131
DENNETT Alexander 4-33, 35
DENOR Richard Sr 4-245
DENOR'S CHOYCE 4-245
DENTON Henry 2-121; Vachell 2-121
DENTON HOLME 2-121
DERBY 3-75
DERUMPLE James 4-19, 37
DESS 4-173
DEVIDEING POINT(See also Dividing Point) 3-146
DICKINSON Robert 2-152; Samuel 2-9, 29, 152, 172; Walter 2-82, 133, 152
DICKS - See Dix
DIGES Robert 3-249
DISCOVERY 1-190; 2-133; 3-235, 236
DITO David 4-205
DIVIDING POINT (See also Divideing Point) 3-250
DIX Elizabeth 3-133; 4-40; Robert 3-41, 95, 133; 4-40
DIXON William 2-159

www.ingramcontent.com/pod-product-compliance
Lightning Source LLC
Chambersburg PA
CBHW050541280326
41933CB00011B/1673